Introducing
BASS

by
Stephan Richter

Visit our Website
www.learntoplaymusic.com

The Progressive Series of Music Instruction Books, CDs, and DVDs

CD TRACK LISTING

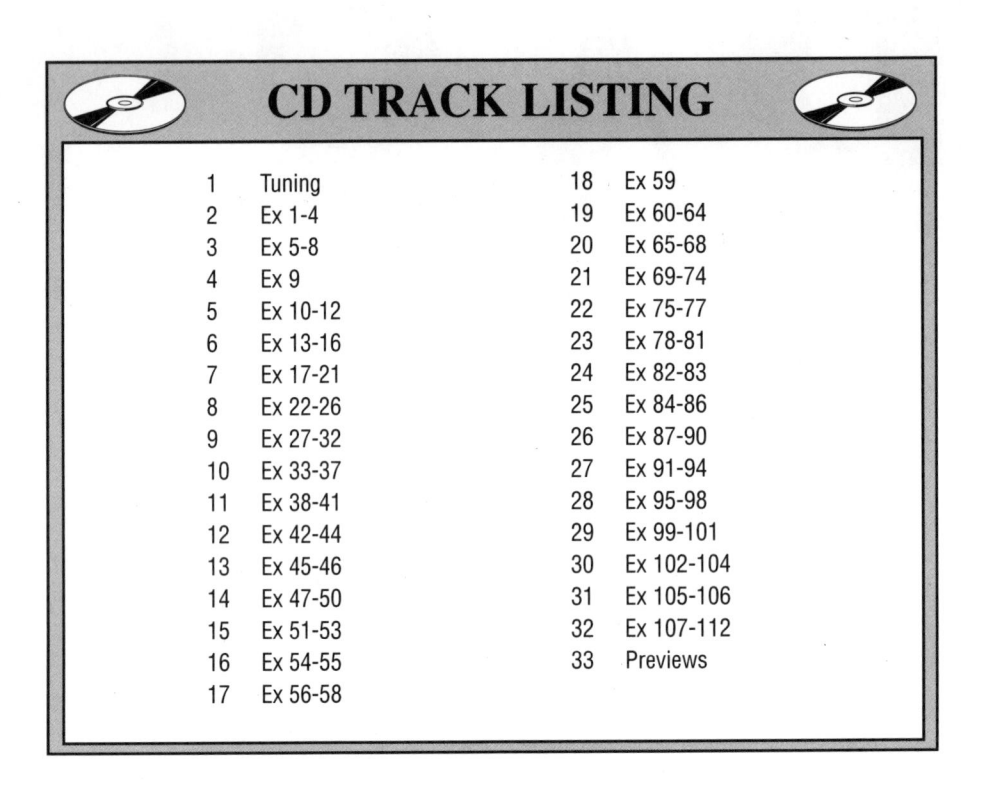

1	Tuning	18	Ex 59
2	Ex 1-4	19	Ex 60-64
3	Ex 5-8	20	Ex 65-68
4	Ex 9	21	Ex 69-74
5	Ex 10-12	22	Ex 75-77
6	Ex 13-16	23	Ex 78-81
7	Ex 17-21	24	Ex 82-83
8	Ex 22-26	25	Ex 84-86
9	Ex 27-32	26	Ex 87-90
10	Ex 33-37	27	Ex 91-94
11	Ex 38-41	28	Ex 95-98
12	Ex 42-44	29	Ex 99-101
13	Ex 45-46	30	Ex 102-104
14	Ex 47-50	31	Ex 105-106
15	Ex 51-53	32	Ex 107-112
16	Ex 54-55	33	Previews
17	Ex 56-58		

INTRODUCING BASS
I.S.B.N. 978 0 947183 88 2
Order Code: CP-18388

Acknowledgments
Photographs: Phil Martin

For more information on this series contact;
L.T.P. Publishing Pty Ltd
email: info@learntoplaymusic.com
or visit our website;
www.learntoplaymusic.com

COPYRIGHT CONDITIONS
No part of this product can be reproduced in any form without the written consent of the publishers.
© 2010 L.T.P. Publishing Pty Ltd
RC-RLER

Published by
KOALA MUSIC PUBLICATIONS™

Contents

Use and Function of Recording
and Metronome 4
Introduction 5
Notation 6
The Bass Guitar 9
Playing Position....................................10
Fretboard Diagram 11
Open String Notes 11
Bass Technique 12
The Right Hand 13
Anchoring of the Thumb 13
Playing with the Fingers 13
Single Finger Stroke 14
The Quarter Note 14
Playing with the Pick............................15
Playing with Alternating Fingers 15
Quarter Note Rest 16
12 Bar Blues 17
The Left Hand 19
Notes on the Second Fret 19
Notes on the Third Fret 21
Half Notes 23
Dotted Half Notes 25
Eighth Notes 26
Whole Note 27
New Note on the E String (F) 28
New Notes on the G String (B, C) 30
The Major Scale 31
The Octave 31
Chromatic Scale, Sharps and Flats 33

Staccato 35
Riffs 36
Chords and Arpeggios 37
Arpeggio Patterns (major) 39
Shifting Between Chords......................40
First and Second Endings 40
The 12 Bar Blues Progression 41
12 Bar Riff..42
Riff Variations 44
Arpeggio Patterns (minor)....................45
Chord Progression 46
The Dotted Quarter Note 48
The Tie 49
Eighth Note Rest 50
Lead In..51
Natural 51
Syncopation 52
Eighth Note Triplets 54
Shuffle Rhythm 54
The Quarter Note Triplet 57
The Slide 58
Sixteenth Notes 59
The Hammer-on 60
The Slap Technique 62
The Tapping Technique........................62
Appendix: Tuning 63
The Bass Guitar 65
The Bass Amp System 66
Sounds and Effects 67
Playing in a Band 68

Use and Function of Recording and Metronome

The Recording

The recording has two functions:

1. As an indication of how the example should sound, and
2. By using as indicated, it gives you the opportunity to play along with another musical instrument. Part of any music practice is to play along with other instruments.

You may have to practice the exercises at a slower speed before attempting to play along with the recording. The metronome then, is useful as you can adjust it to the speed you want.

The Metronome

A metronome is a mechanical or electronic device that divides time into equal beats by producing a ticking or bleeping sound. The number of beats per minute is adjustable so that you can vary the speed at which you wish to play a piece of music.

The metronome has three functions:

1. It indicates what tempo a tune should be played at by sounding the number of beats per minute.

    e.g. ♩ = 60: in this case it tells us that a beat (quarter note) is exactly one second.

2. It acts as a control for your timing so that you don't rush or slow down during your playing.

3. It helps you by gradually increasing the tempo on the number scale until you can play at the desired speed.

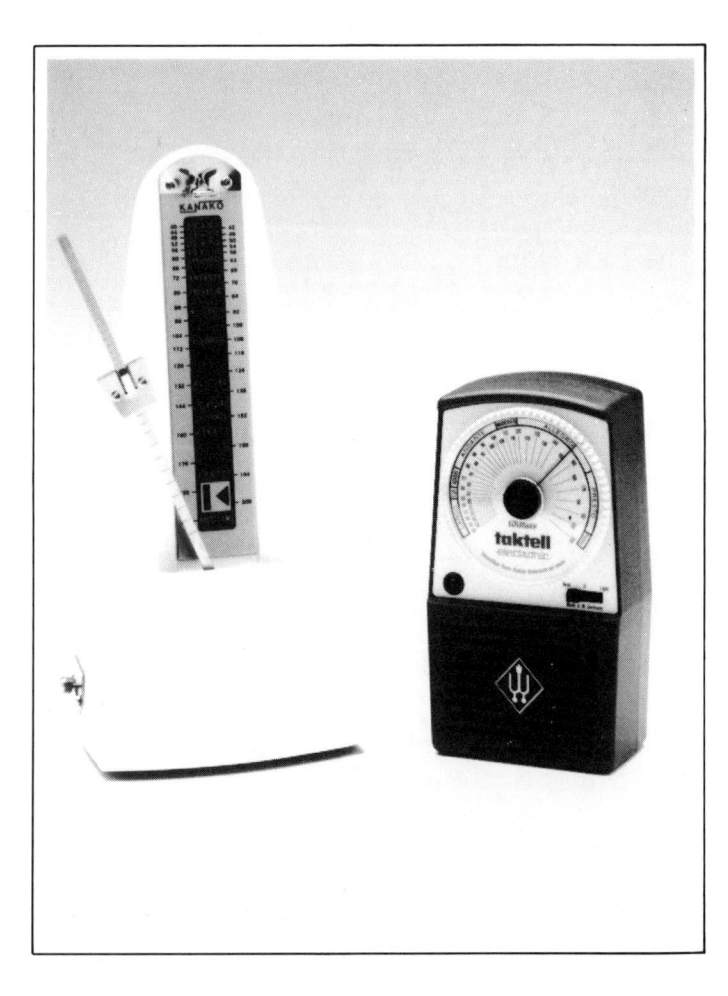

Introduction

This book introduces the beginner to the basics of playing bass guitar. No previous knowledge of bass guitar playing or music is required. All techniques and music theory are gradually introduced in a very easy and clear way using over 110 examples, riffs and licks. You do not need to read music to use this book, however, both music and tablature notation are used to show the position of the notes on the fretboard. A metronome or a drum machine is suggested to help you develop your rhythm and keep time. The emphasis of this book is to get the student to play interesting music on the bass, and even the early exercises sound great!

It is recommended that you use the recording that is available for this book. It contains all the examples within, and you will learn faster when you are able to hear what the example sounds like and play along with the backing band. As the bass player is part of the rhythm section, it is essential to play together as often and as soon as possible with other instruments, especially drums. Chord symbols are placed above some examples so that a guitarist can play along with the bass guitar.

It is important to have a correct approach to practice. You will benefit more from several short practices (e.g. 15-30 minutes per day) than one or two long sessions per week. This is especially so in the early stages, because of the basic nature of the material being studied. In a practice session you should divide your time evenly between the study of new material and the revision of past work. It is a common mistake for semi-advanced students to practice only the pieces they can already play well. Although this is more enjoyable, it is not a very satisfactory method of practice. You should also endeavour to correct mistakes and experiment with new ideas.

You should combine the study of this book with constant experimentation and listening to other players. It is the author's belief that the guidance of an experienced teacher will be an invaluable aid in your progress.

Stephan Richter obtained his degree in Classical Music (Cello major) at the Zurich Conservatorium of Music in Switzerland. He further studied in New York on Electric Bass with Rick Laird and Tony Oppenheim. He currently works as a session musician and teacher. Stephan is author of Progressive Slap Technique for Bass, Tapping Technique for Bass, Heavy Metal Method and Heavy Metal Techniques for Bass, Heavy Metal Licks Volume 1 and 2 and Progressive Bass Guitar Licks.

NOTATION

Two methods of music notation are presented in this book; namely notes and tablature. You need only use one of these methods*, whichever is most convenient (if you are not familiar with note reading follow the tablature outlined below).

Tablature

Tablature is a method of indicating the position of notes on the fretboard. There are four "tab" lines, each representing one of the four strings on the bass.

1 Thinnest
2
3 STRINGS
4 Thickest

NUT

When a number is placed on one of the lines, it indicates the fret location of a note, e.g.

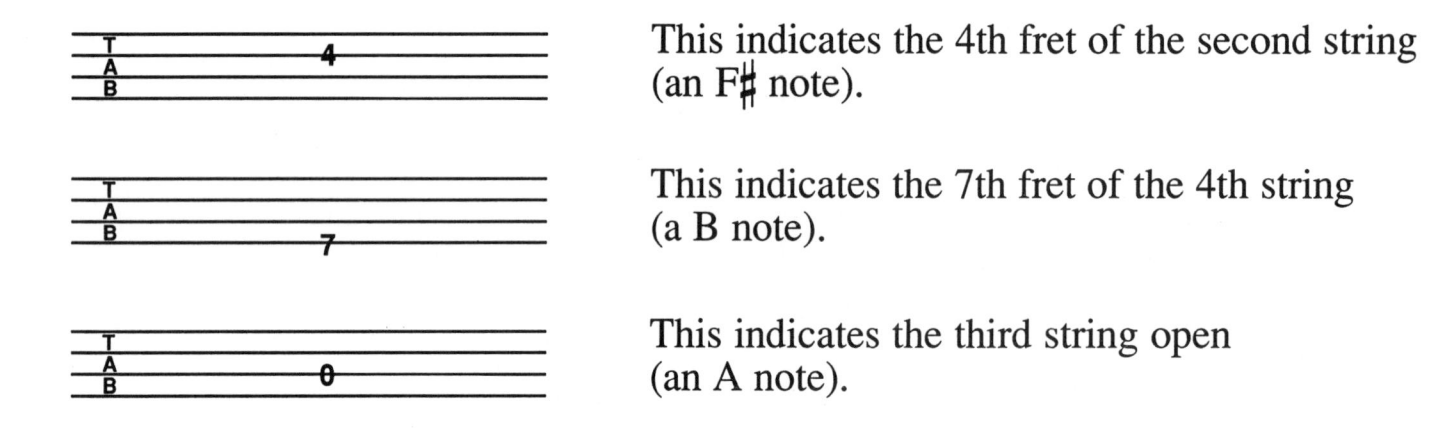

This indicates the 4th fret of the second string (an F♯ note).

This indicates the 7th fret of the 4th string (a B note).

This indicates the third string open (an A note).

The tablature, as used in this book, does not indicate the time values of the notes, only their position on the fretboard. You can read the time values by following the count written beneath the tablature, e.g.

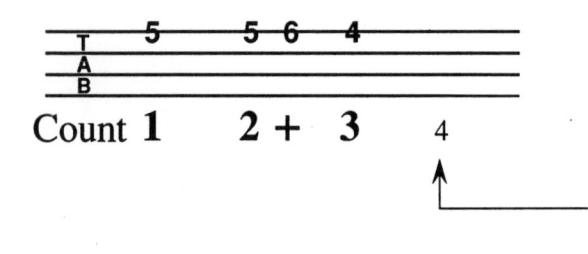

Count 1   2 + 3   4

In this example the 1st note is worth 1 count, the 2nd and 3rd notes are worth half a count each and the 4th note is worth 2 counts.

The small number in the count is used to indicate where a note is being held or where a rest occurs.

*Note readers may need to refer to the tablature to determine the position of an exercise.

Music Notation

The musical alphabet consists of 7 letters: A B C D E F G

Music is written on a staff, which consists of 5 parallel lines between which there are 4 spaces.

Music Staff

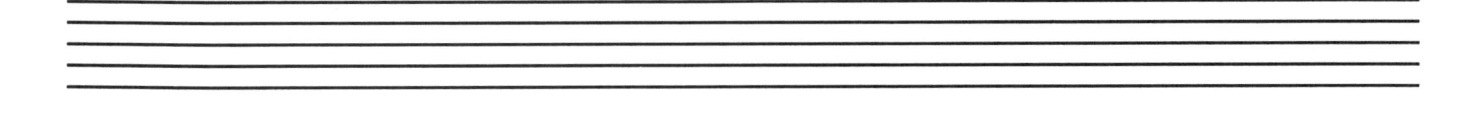

The Bass clef sign is placed at the beginning of each staff line.

Bass Clef →

This clef indicates the position of the note F which is on the line in between the two dots, (it is an old fashioned method of writing the letter F).

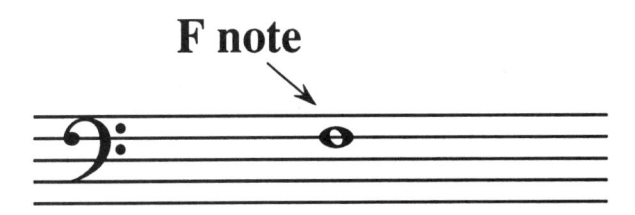

F note

The other lines and spaces on the staff are named as such:

Extra notes can be added by the use of short lines, called leger lines:

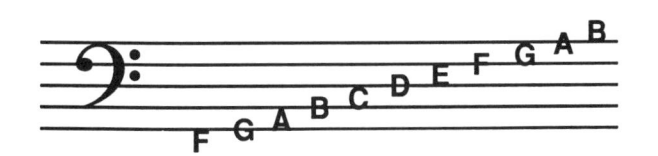

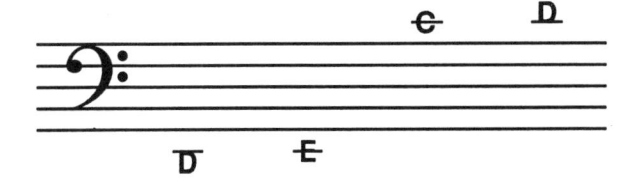

When a note is placed on the staff its head indicates its position, e.g:

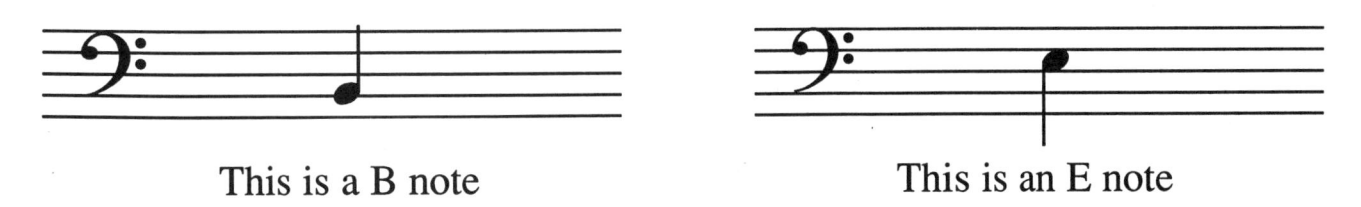

This is a B note

This is an E note

When the note head is below the middle staff line the stem points upward and when the head is above the middle line the stem points downward. A note placed on the middle line (D) can have its stem pointing either up or down.

Bar lines are drawn across the staff, to divide the music into sections called Bars or Measures. A double bar line signifies either the end of the music, or the end of an important section of it.

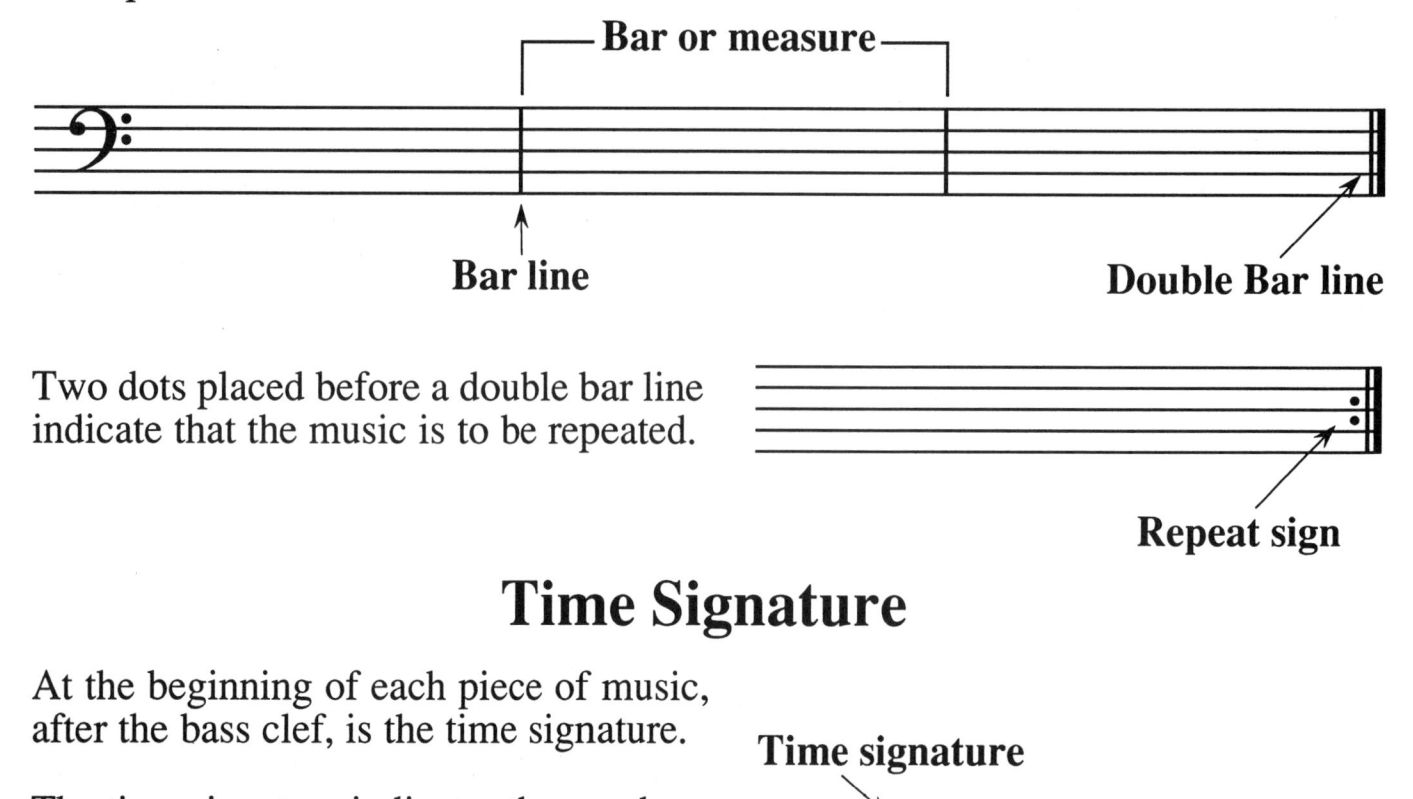

Two dots placed before a double bar line indicate that the music is to be repeated.

Time Signature

At the beginning of each piece of music, after the bass clef, is the time signature.

The time signature indicates the number of beats per bar (the top number) and the type of note receiving one beat (the bottom number). For example:

4 - this indicates 4 beats per bar.
4 - this indicates that each beat is worth a quarter note (crotchet).

Thus in 4/4 time there must be the equivalent of 4 quarter note beats per bar.

The Bass Guitar

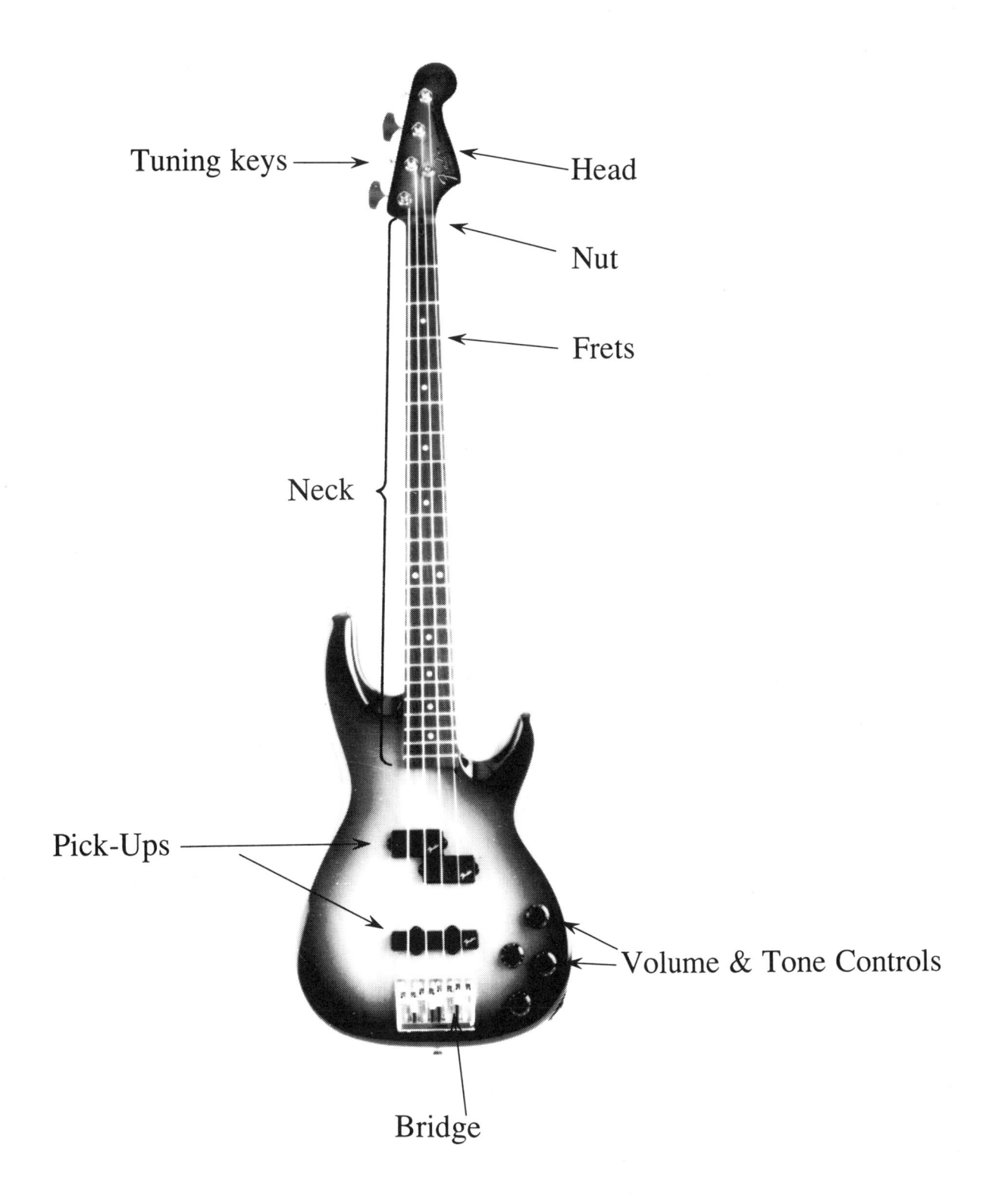

Playing Position

To have a comfortable playing position, it is best to use a strap. A wide strap, approx. 2–3 inches (8–10cm) is best, so the weight of the bass is evenly distributed. Adjust the strap to a length that is comfortable. The full weight of the bass should be resting on the shoulder strap.

The bass should be angled slightly upwards (see photo), so that your left arm is free to move while you play.

Whether you prefer to sit or to stand while you play, make sure that the position of your bass (strap length and angle) is the same so that your playing won't be affected.

Keep the bass close to your body so that it is easy to reach all parts of it when you play.

① Standing Position

② Sitting Position

Sitting Position:
Sit on a stool with a foot rest to raise your right leg, or just cross your right leg over your left.

Fretboard Diagram

A fretboard diagram is a grid pattern of strings (vertical lines) and frets (horizontal lines) which is used to indicate the position of notes.

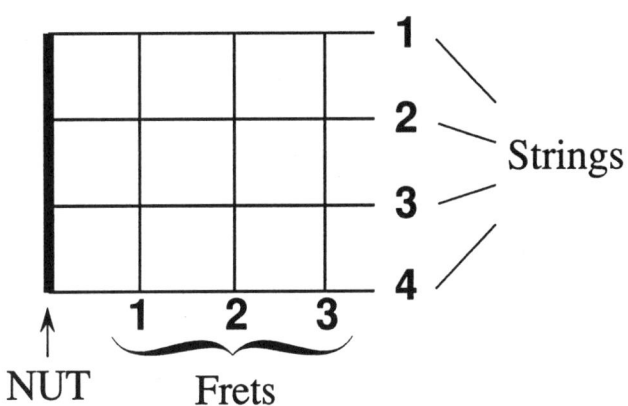

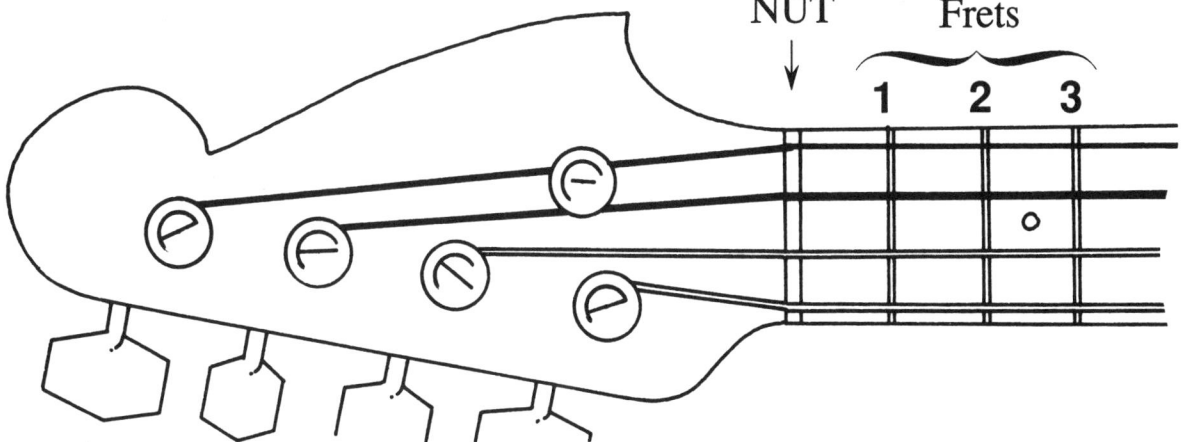

Open String Notes

The following fretboard diagram illustrates the four open string notes of the bass guitar.

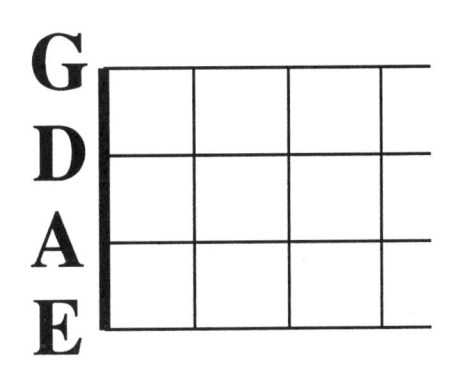

Here are the four open string notes in music and tablature notation.

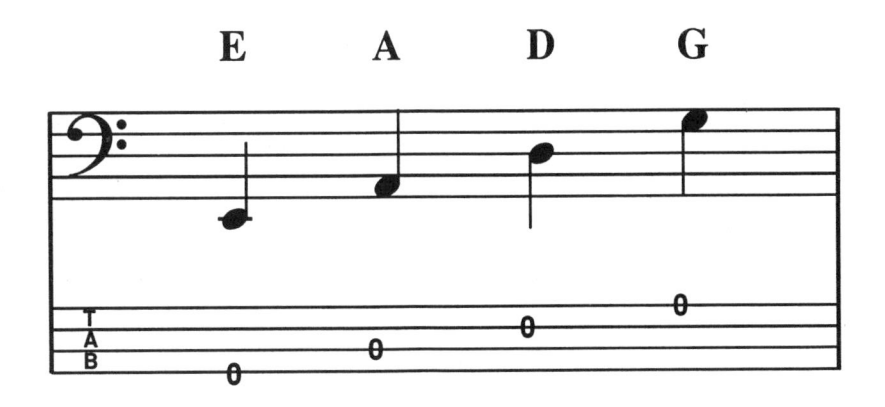

Bass Technique

The Left Hand

The fingers of the left hand are numbered as follows:

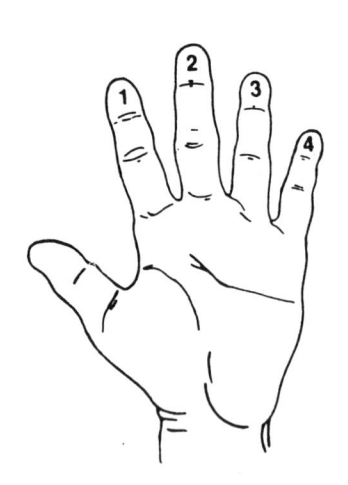

1 = Index finger
2 = Middle finger
3 = Ring finger
4 = Little finger

The Right Hand

The fingers of the right hand are named as follows:

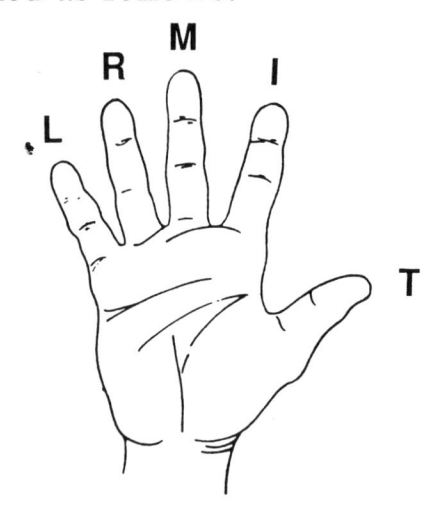

T = Thumb finger
I = Index finger
M = Middle finger
R = Ring finger
L = Little finger

In the more advanced examples there will be an indication of what fingers and technique are used to get the best result and sound effect. Usually the left hand finger number, if needed, is written next to the music note and the technique to be used above or below the note.

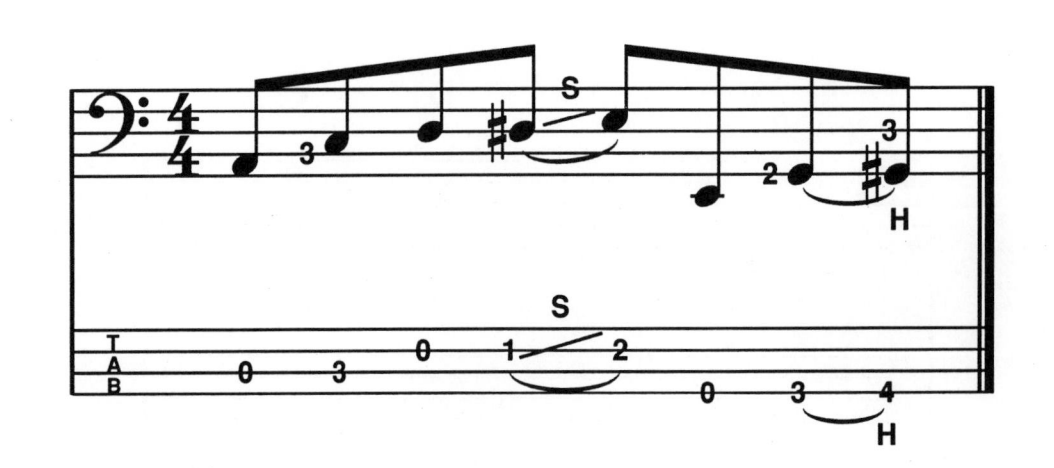

THE RIGHT HAND
Anchoring of the Thumb

To get a steady feel and sound it is important to anchor your hand. The best way of doing this is by placing the thumb on the top of the pick-up (see photo).

Most modern bass guitars have two pick-ups. One close to the fretboard and a second one nearer the bridge. In the early stages of playing it may be easier to place your thumb on the front pick-up as the string tension is not quite as "hard" as on the back pick-up. The tone will also sound fuller and heavier, and it will also be easier for your right hand fingers to play the strings.

You should also experiment by playing with your thumb resting on the back pick-up, as the sound is clearer and has more attack and "bite".

Playing with the Fingers

When playing notes, the rest stroke is used. The rest stroke involves the finger picking the string and then coming to rest on the next string. The photos below illustrate the movement of the index finger in playing the rest stroke. i.e. pick the A string and come to rest on the E string.

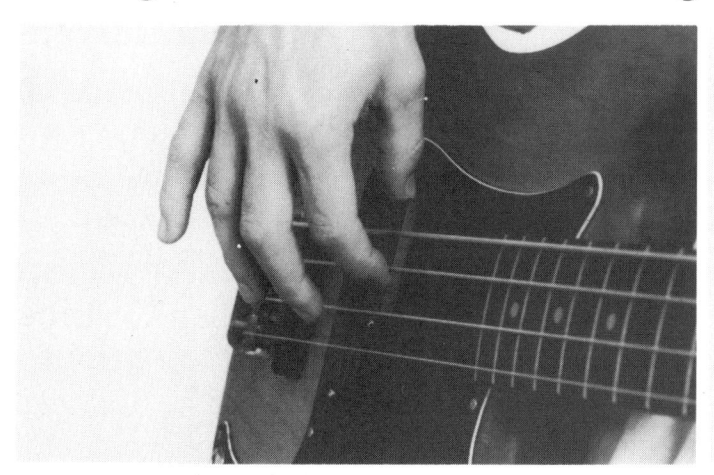

Single Finger Stroke

Anchor your thumb on a pick-up and play the open third string with your right hand index finger (I). You are playing an A note using what is called the single stroke technique.

The Quarter Note

The notes you are playing are called quarter notes (♩). There are four quarter notes in each bar of 4/4 time.

1.

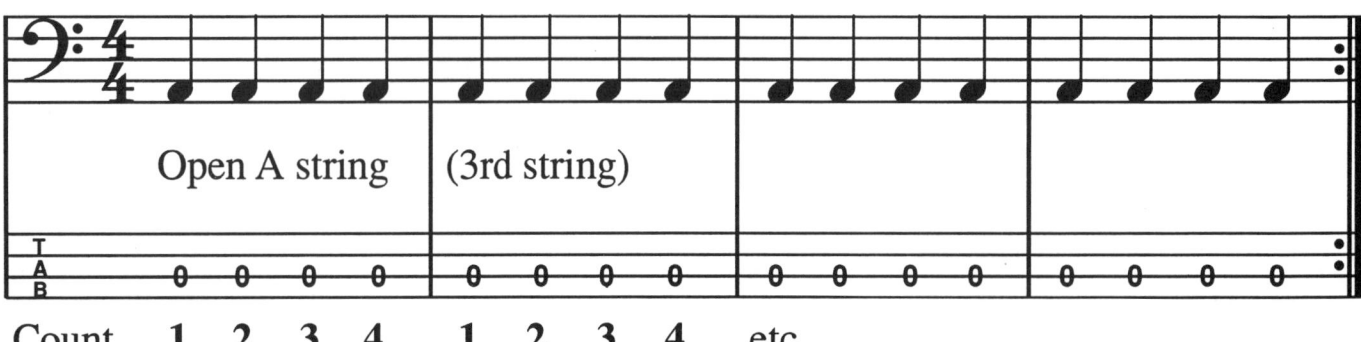

Open A string | (3rd string)

Count   1 2 3 4   1 2 3 4   etc.

Repeat the above exercise using your right hand middle finger.

The next three examples use the right hand single stroke technique on the three remaining open strings. You can use either your index or middle finger.

2.

Open D string (2nd string)

3.

Open E string (4th string)

4.

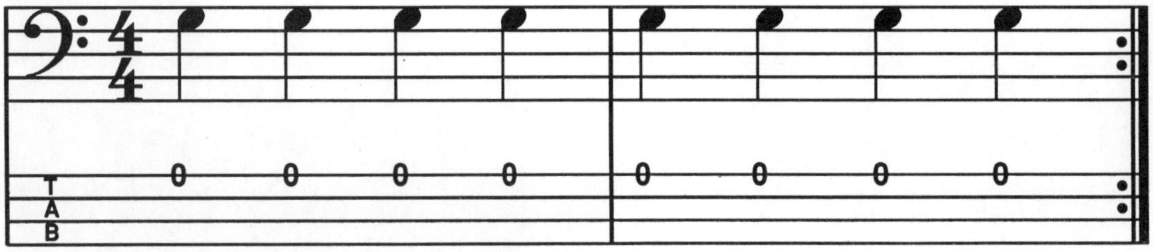

Open G string (1st string)

Playing with the Pick

Picks are usually made of plastic and come in a variety of different shapes and thicknesses. Most bass players prefer a medium or thick gauge pick, as thin picks tend to give a less defined sound.

The pick is held between the thumb and index finger, as illustrated in the photographs below:

Many bass players use this picking grip.

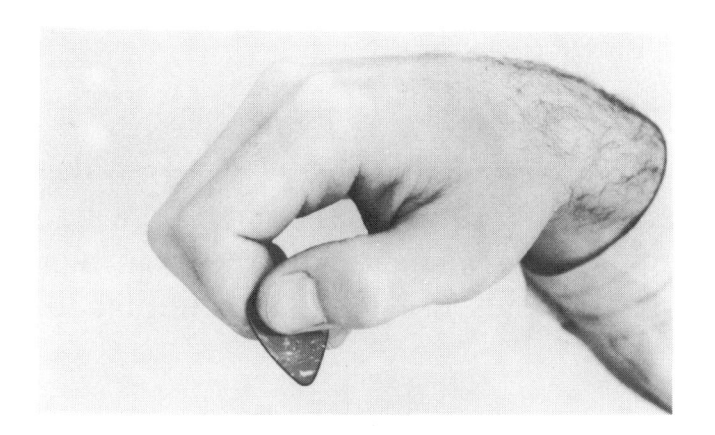

Play each note in Examples One to Four using a downward pick motion. Use only the tip of the pick. When playing with the pick move your hand from the wrist. Do not keep it rigid.

Playing with Alternating Fingers

Alternate between your index and middle fingers. Anchor your thumb on the pick-up and strike the open G string with your index finger in the same fashion as with the single stroke technique. As soon as it comes to rest on the next lower string (D string) pick the open G string again, this time using your middle finger. Maintain this alternating movement between the two fingers. Make sure one of the two fingers is always resting on the D string while the other one is picking the G string and vice versa.

Always use this alternating finger style as it will give you more possibilities when changing between notes and strings.

Go back to the previous examples and use the alternating finger style.

Quarter Note Rest

A quarter note rest is a beat of silence. In the example below there is a rest on the fourth beat of each bar. To obtain this silence you must stop the strings from vibrating (i.e. muting them). This is achieved by placing your left hand fingers lightly on the strings. Do not press too hard as this will produce a new note. When using the left hand to mute an open string, place it over all four strings as this is easier (see photo).

5.

Count   **1 2 3** 4   **1 2 3** 4

When changing strings e.g. from the open G string down to the open D string, you have to use the left hand to mute the G string, otherwise there will be two strings sounding at the same time. In the following examples use left hand muting to achieve each rest.

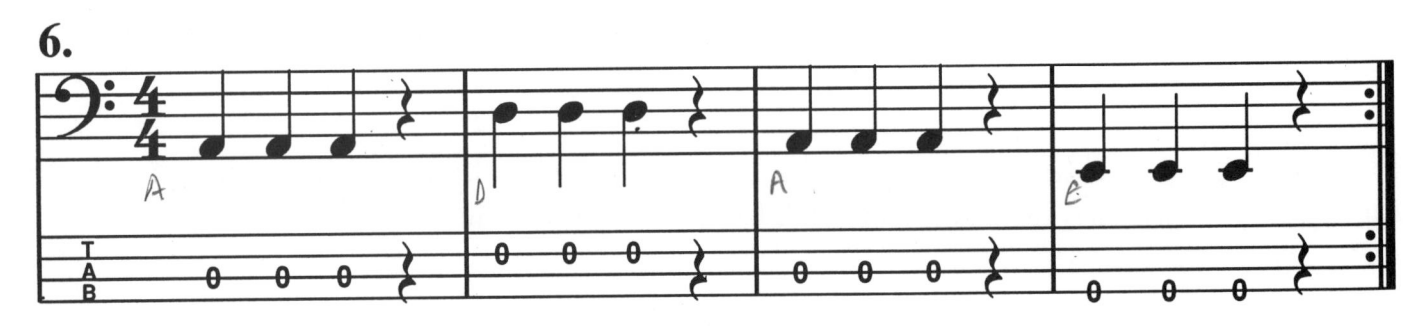

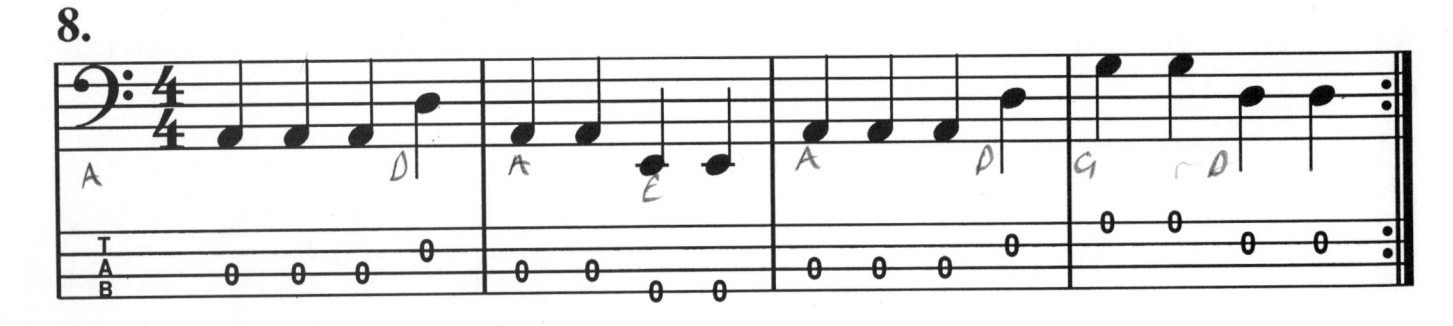

6.

7.

8.

12 Bar Blues

12 bar blues is a pattern of chords which repeats every 12 bars. This progression is invaluable to the bass guitarist because of its use in many songs. For example, songs performed by Elvis Presley, Chuck Berry and the Beatles, such as "Hound Dog", "Johnny B. Goode" and "Roll Over Beethoven" are all based upon a 12 bar progression.

Example 9 uses a **root note** bass for each chord. A root note is the note with the same name as the chord and will always blend well with that chord.

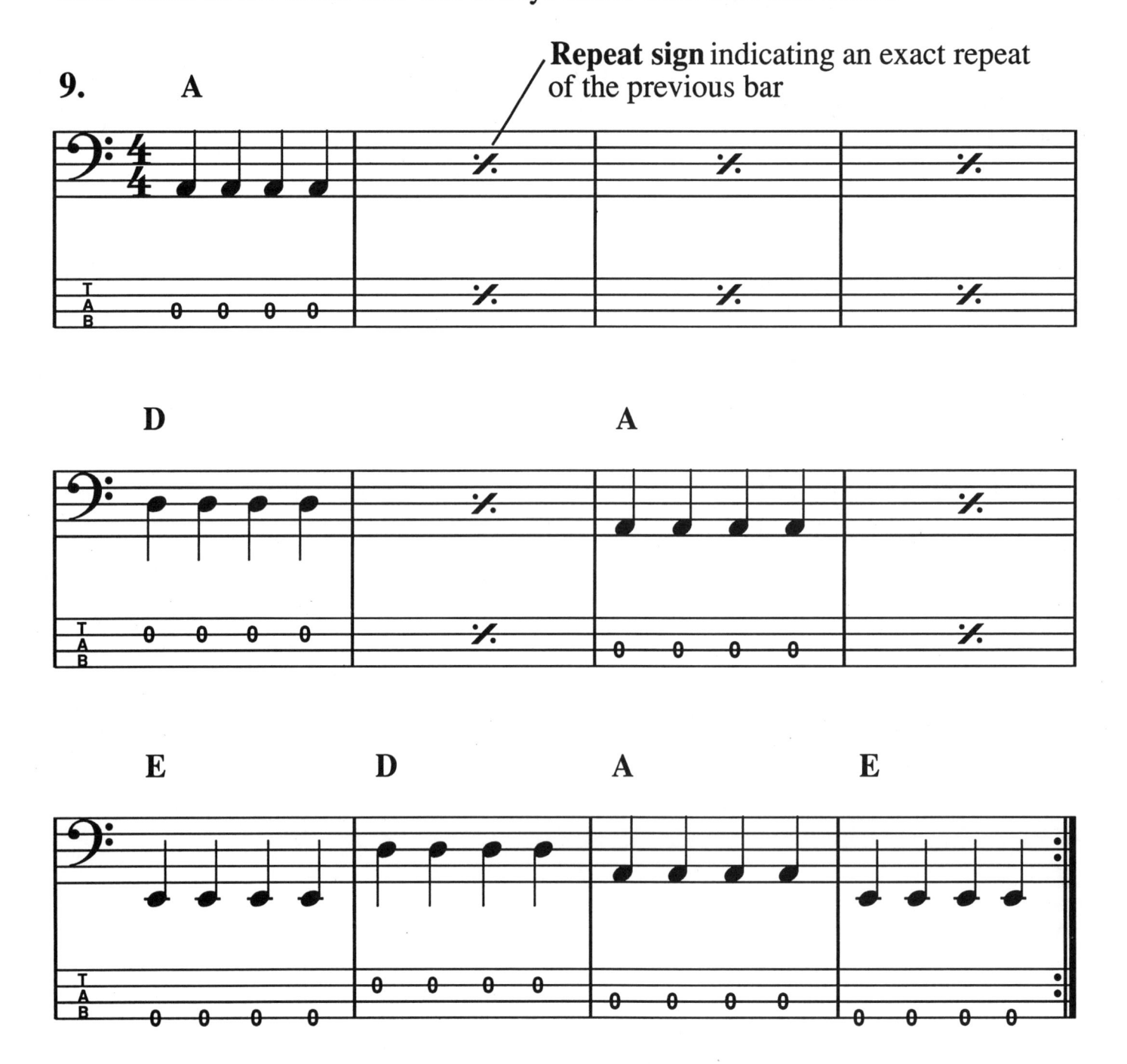

9. A

Repeat sign indicating an exact repeat of the previous bar

D   A

E   D   A   E

Finish the progression with an A note held for four counts.

LEFT HAND

Place the first finger of your left hand just behind the second fret of the G string. This note is an A note. Play this new note with your right hand index finger. Listen to the sound. It should sound full and round. If it buzzes or rattles you have not placed your left hand finger close enough to the fret or you are not pressing the string down hard enough.

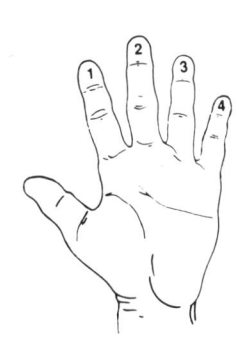

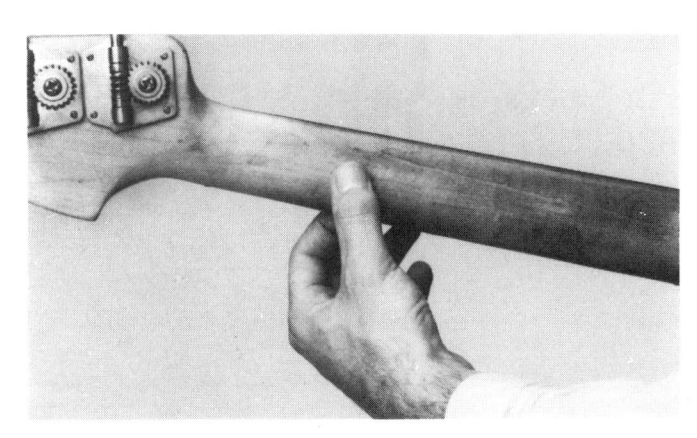

For greater support the left hand thumb should be placed behind the neck of the bass guitar, approximately opposite your index and middle fingers as shown in the photo above.

Notes on the Second Fret

First string (G String)

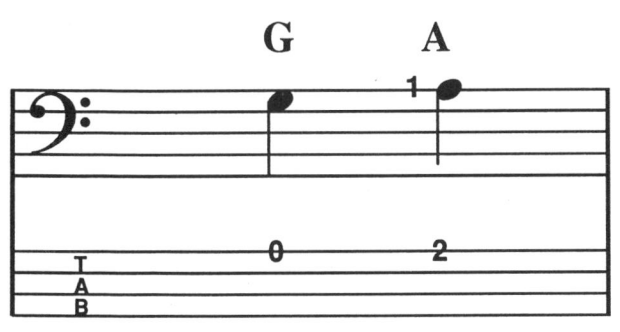

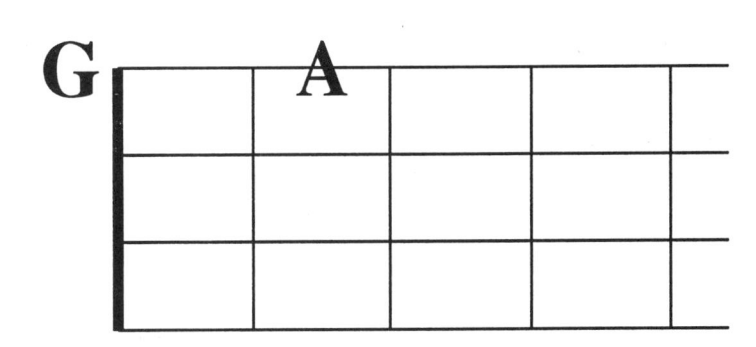

Second string (D string)

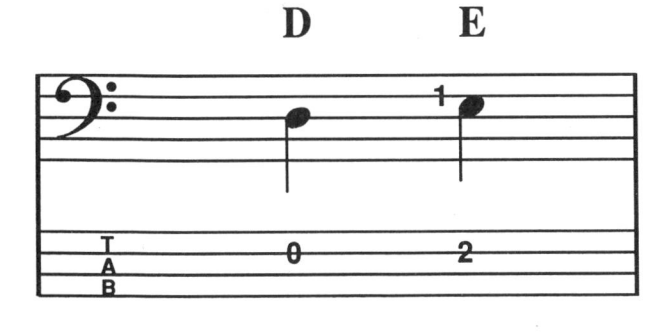

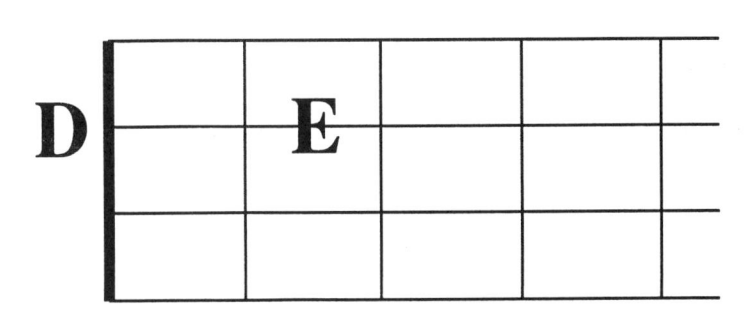

Third string (A string)

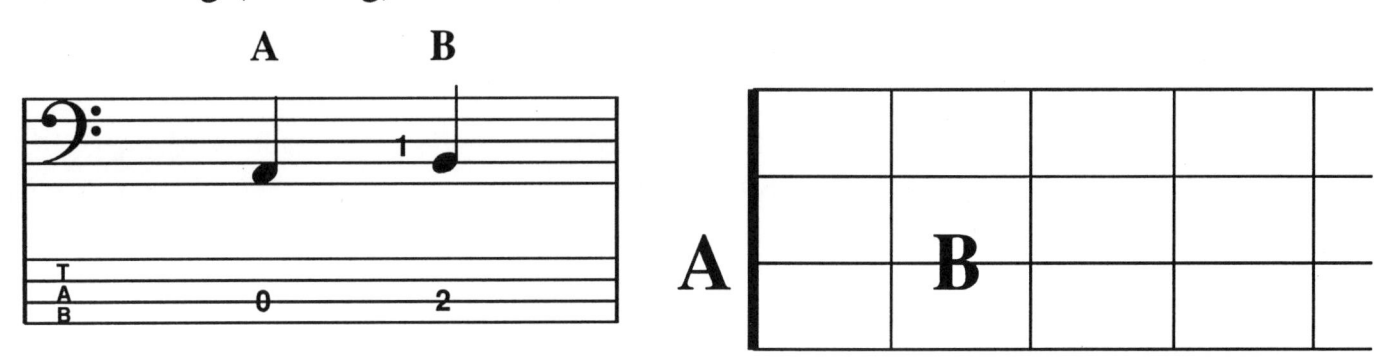

Play these new notes with the first finger of your left hand and the index and middle fingers (alternating) of your right hand.

Memorize these new notes and play them in the following examples.

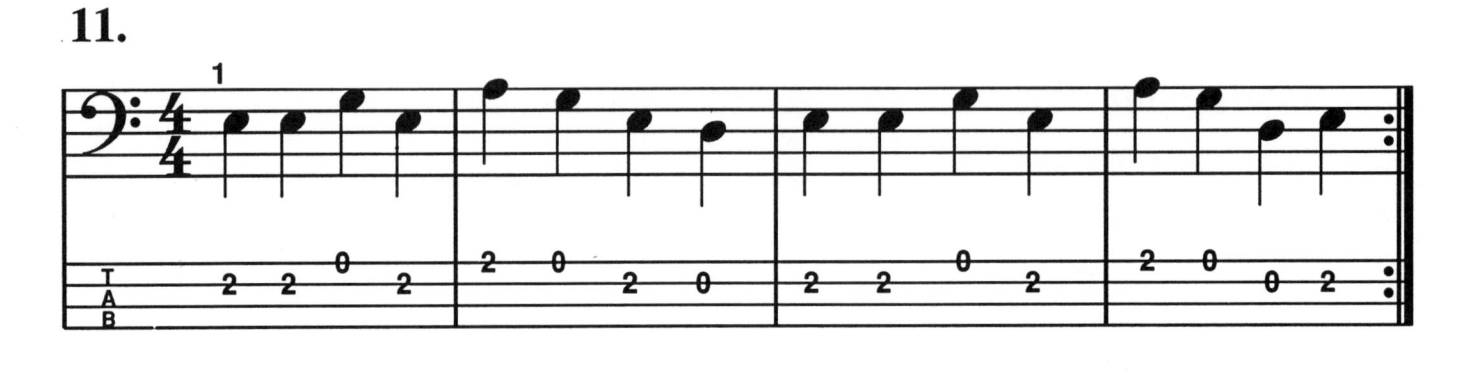

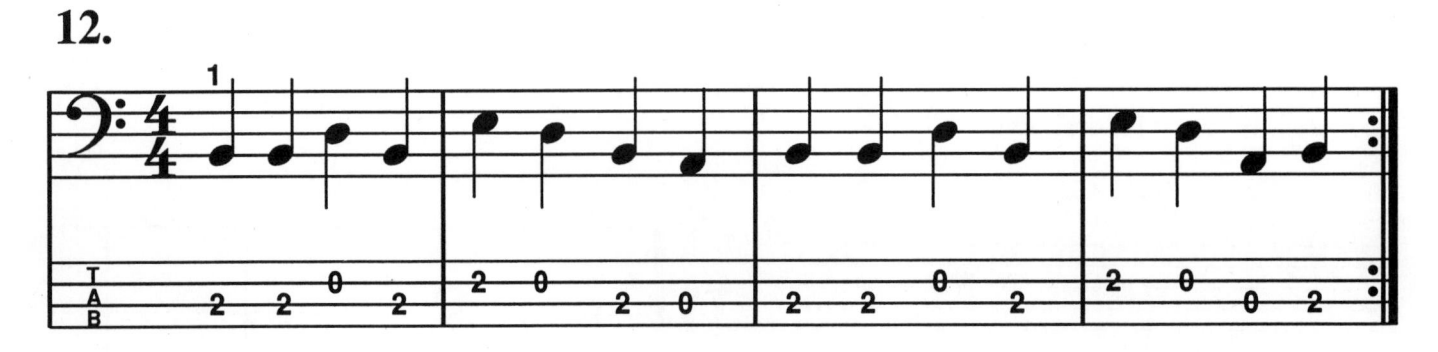

10.

11.

12.

Note that these last two examples have the same pattern but are played on different strings. This is called transposition (transposing).

Notes on the Third Fret

Second string (D string)

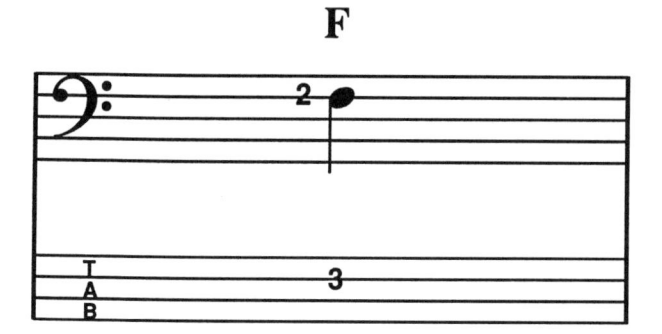

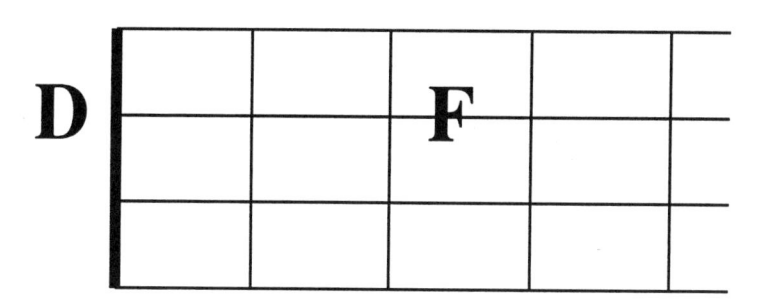

F

Third string (A string)

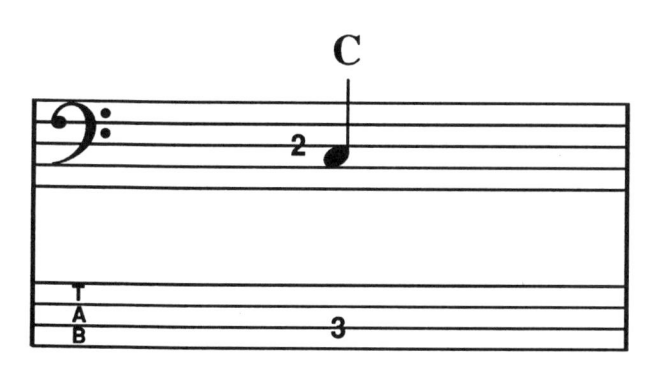

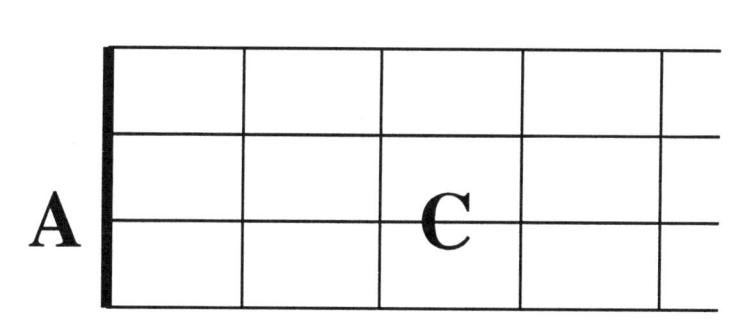

C

Fourth string (E string)

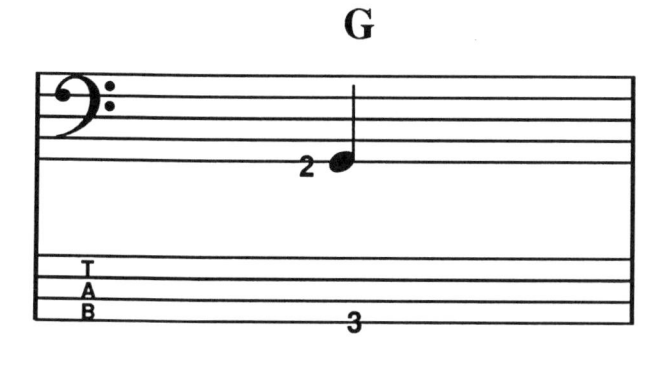

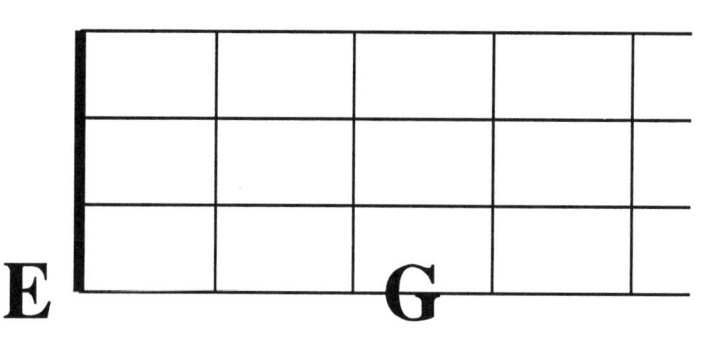

G

Play these new notes with the second finger of your left hand and the index and middle fingers (alternating) of your right hand.

Example 13 uses open strings and first and second finger notes.

13.

Example 14 is transposed down one string from the above example.

14.

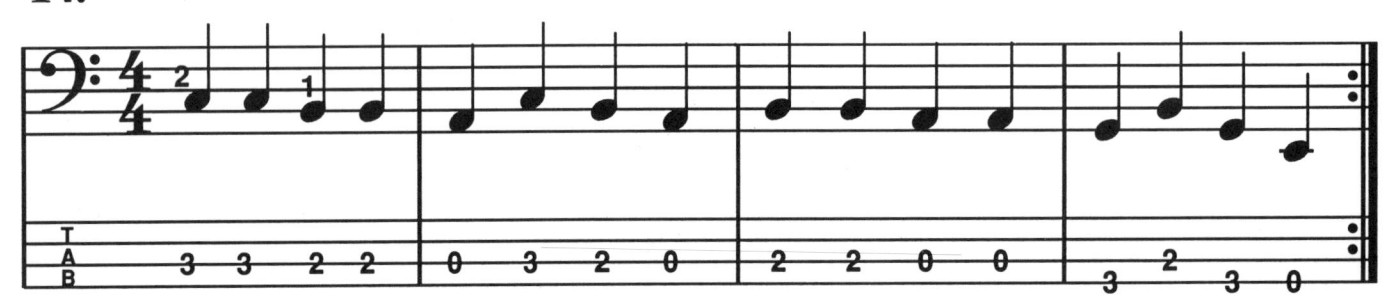

15.

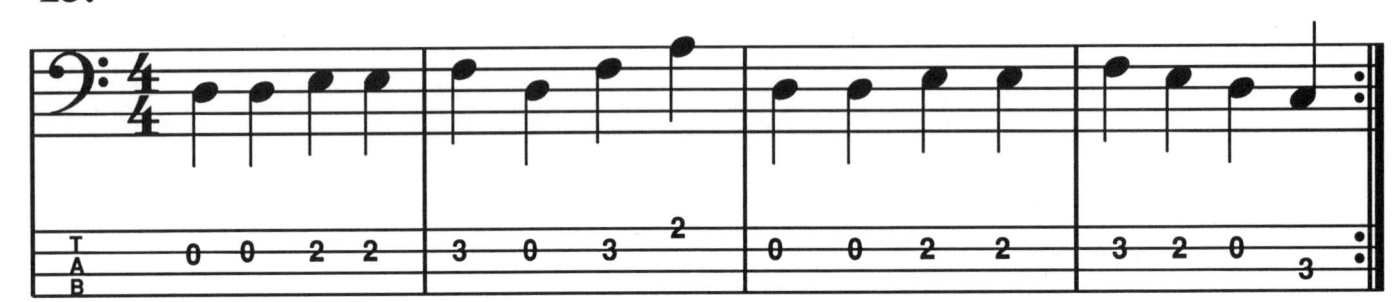

16.

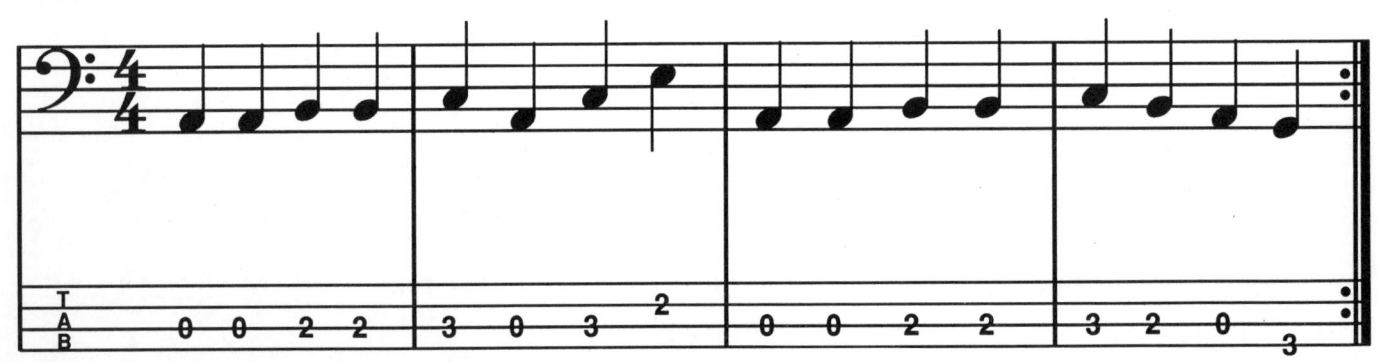

Example 15 and 16 are transpositions of each other.

Half Notes

So far only quarter notes have been used. The next example uses half notes which last for two beats.

17.

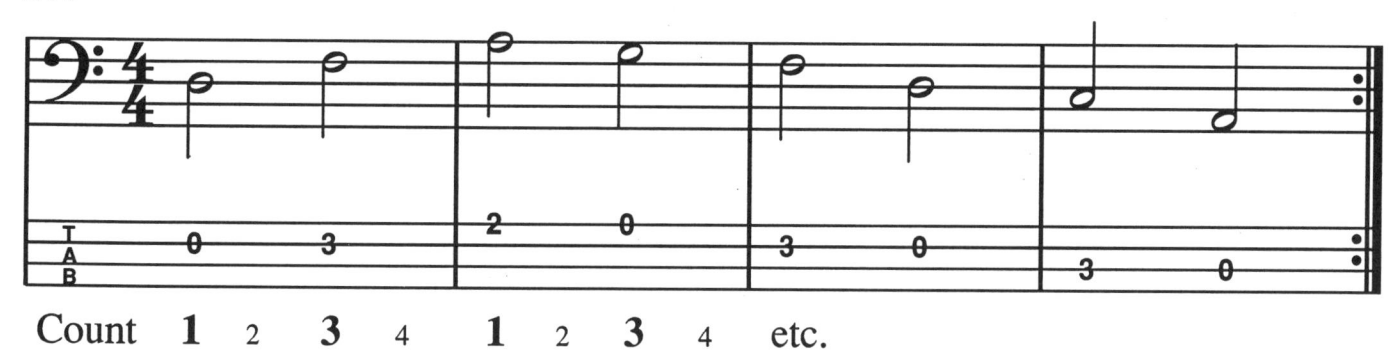

Count   1   2   3   4   1   2   3   4   etc.

18.

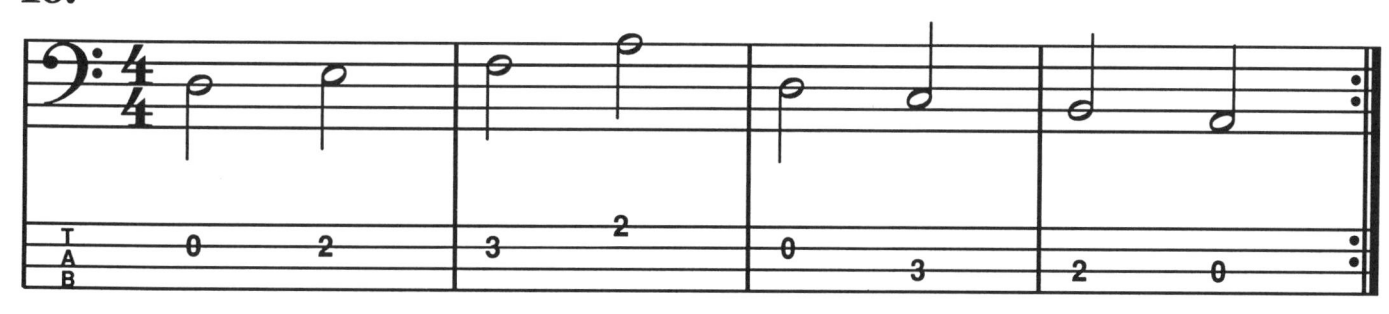

The next three examples use quarter and half notes. Make sure you play the correct length of each note.

19.

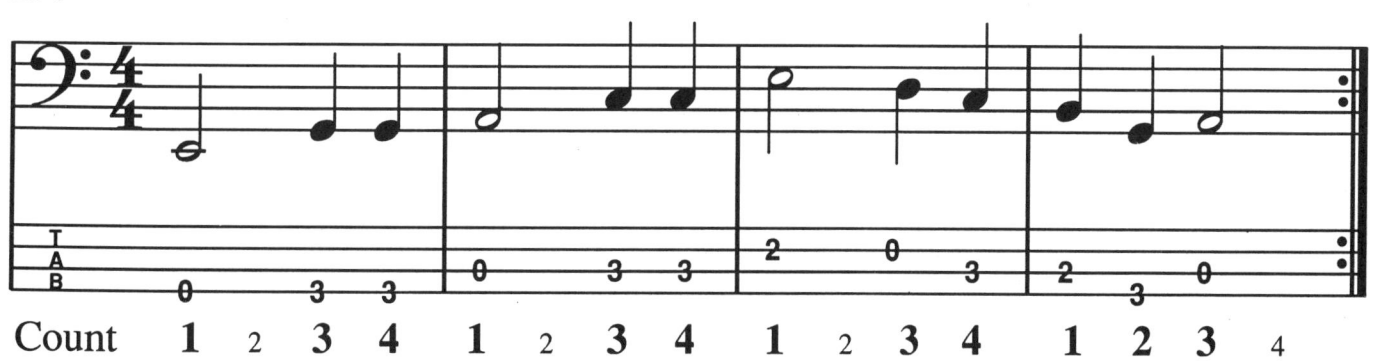

Count   1   2   3   4   1   2   3   4   1   2   3   4   1   2   3   4

20.

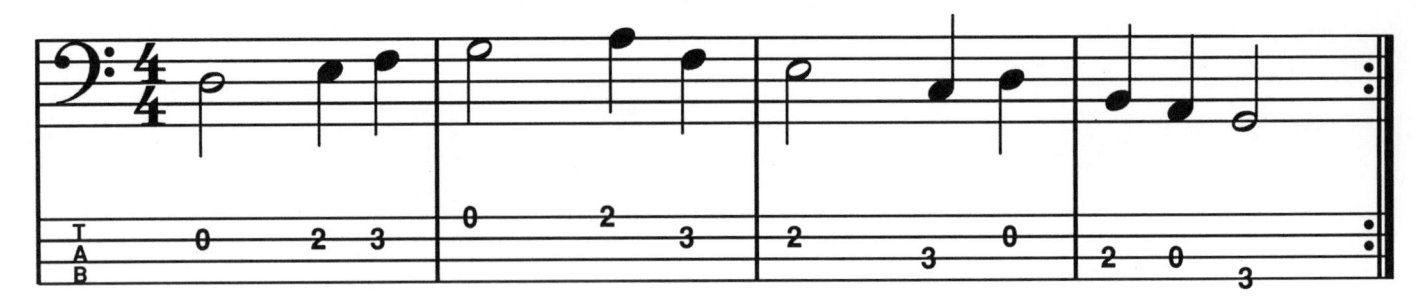

21.

The next two examples use quarter note rests in addition to the quarter notes and half notes (see p. 16).

22.

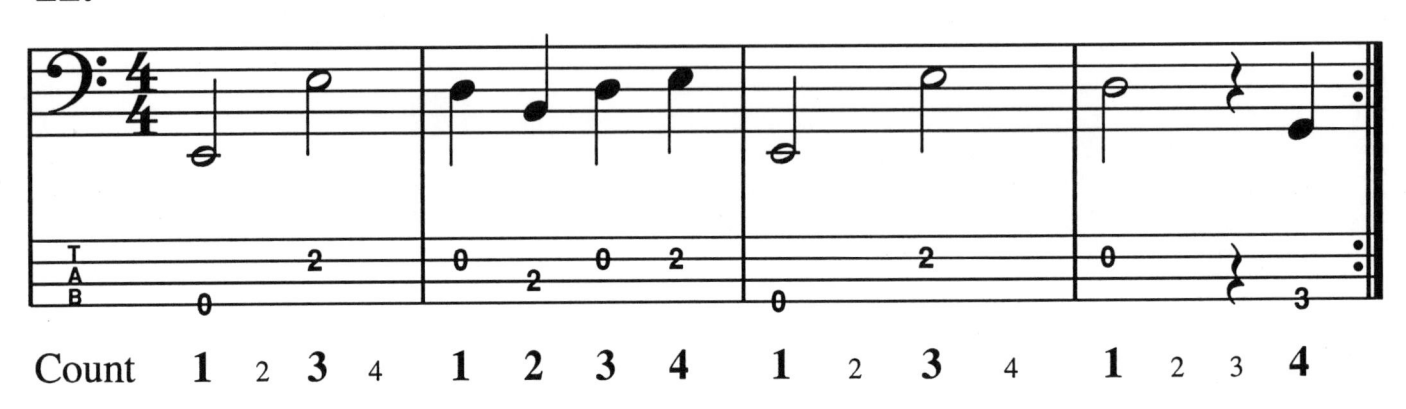

Count   1   2   3   4   **1**   **2**   **3**   **4**   **1**   2   **3**   4   **1**   2   3   **4**

23.

Count   1   2   3   4   **1**   **2**   **3**   4   1   2   **3**   **4**   **1**   **2**   3   **4**

Dotted Half Notes

A dotted half note is worth three beats. When a dot is placed after a note it indicates that its time value is extended by half e.g:

$\textnormal{\textonehalfnote} = 2$ beats $\textnormal{\textonehalfnote.} = 3$ beats

24.

Count   1   2   3   **4**   1   2   3   **4**   etc.

25.

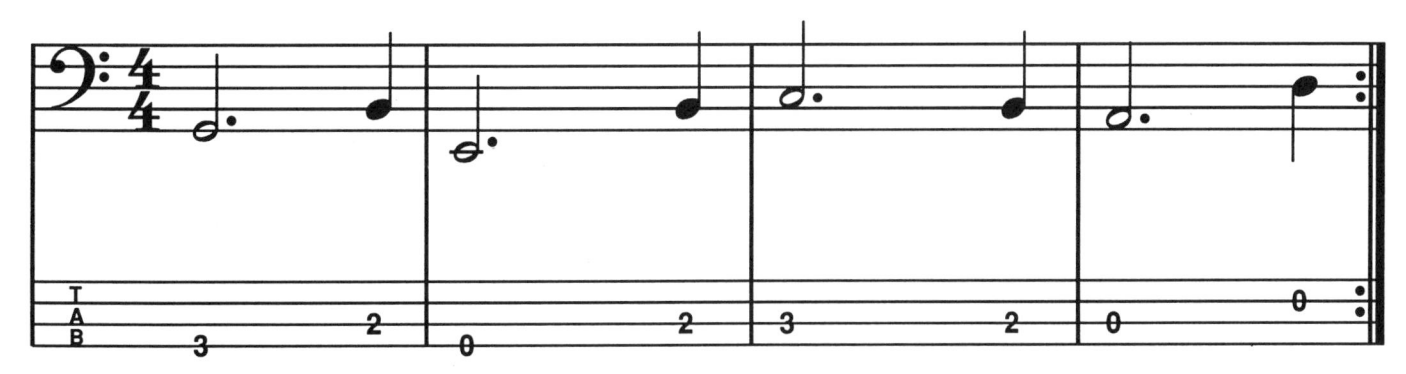

Example 26 combines dotted half notes with half notes and quarter notes.

26.

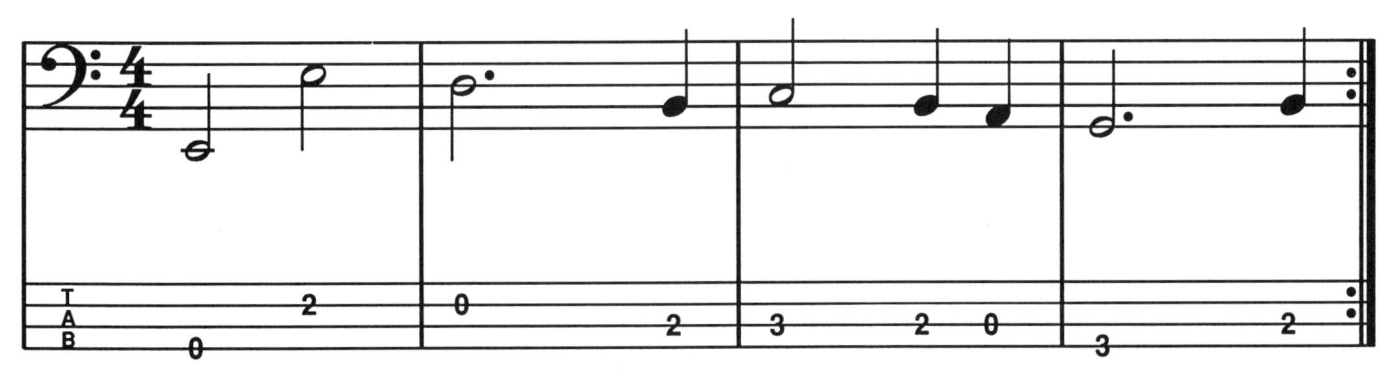

Count   **1**   2   **3**   4   **1**   2   3   **4**   etc.

Eighth Notes

An eighth note (♪) is worth half a beat.

Two eighth notes, which are usually joined by a bar ♫ have the same value as a quarter note. Eighth notes are counted as such:

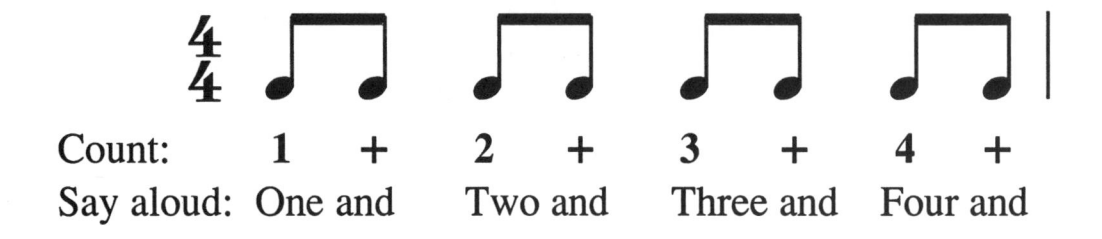

Count: 1 + 2 + 3 + 4 +
Say aloud: One and Two and Three and Four and

The next two examples use eighth notes only.

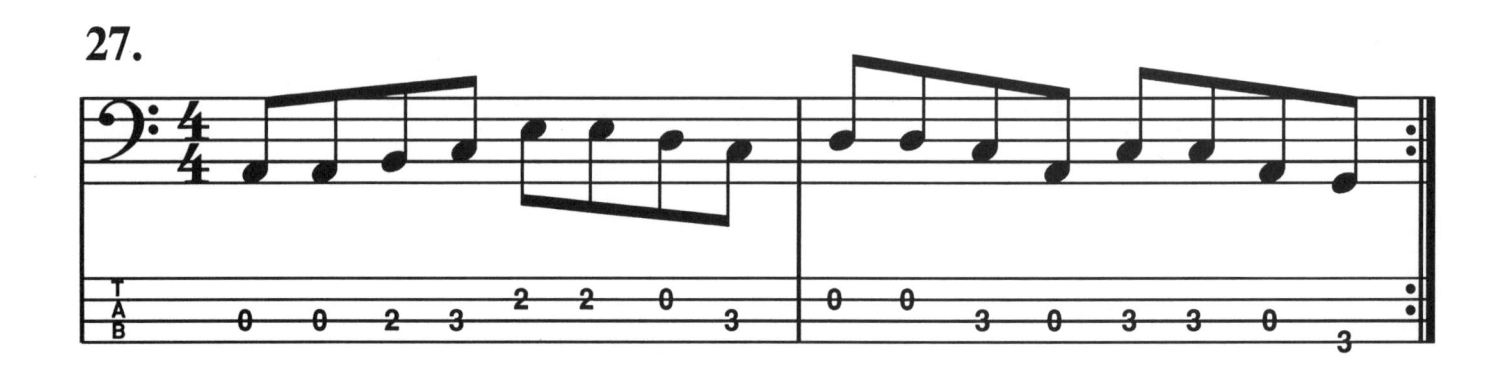

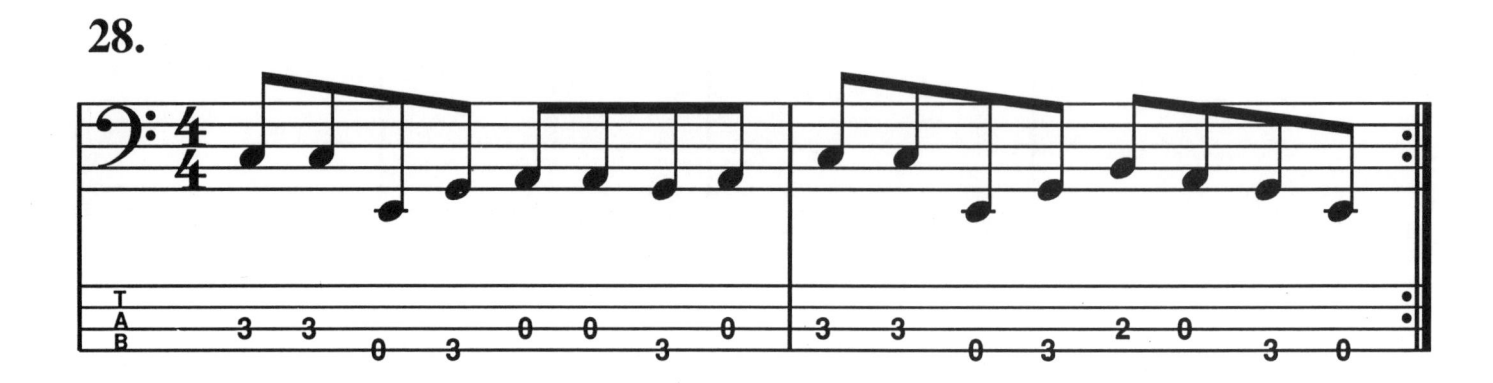

27.

28.

The example below uses quarter notes and eighth notes.

29.

Count   1   2 + 3   4 +   1   2 + 3 + 4 +

The next example uses all the different note values learnt so far.

30.

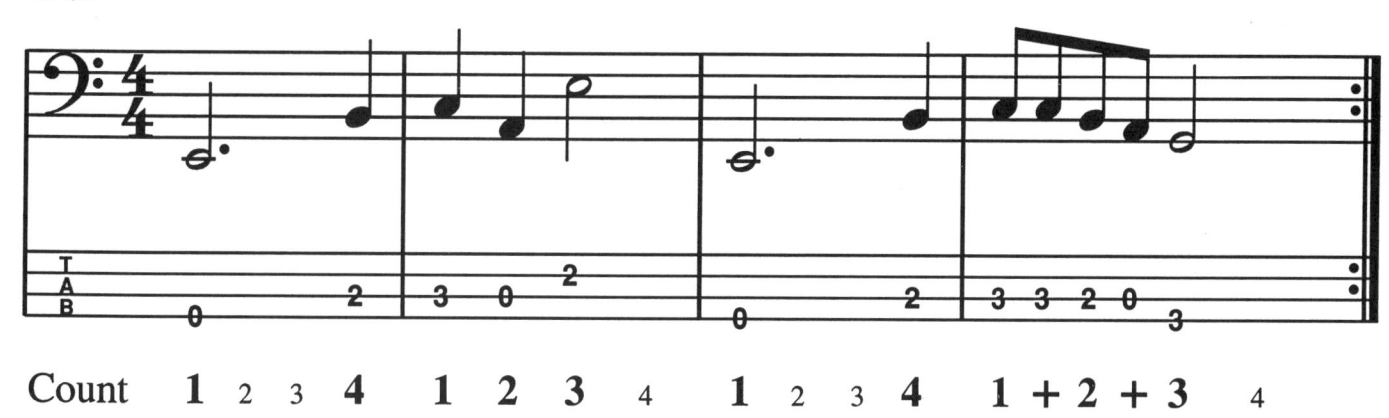

Count   **1** 2 3 **4**   **1** **2** **3** 4   **1** 2 3 **4**   **1 + 2 + 3** 4

31.

O Whole Note

A note with the value of four beats (quarter notes) in one bar of $\frac{4}{4}$ time.
In the last bar there is a whole note lasting for four beats (the whole bar).

32. Am   Dm   Am   Em   Am

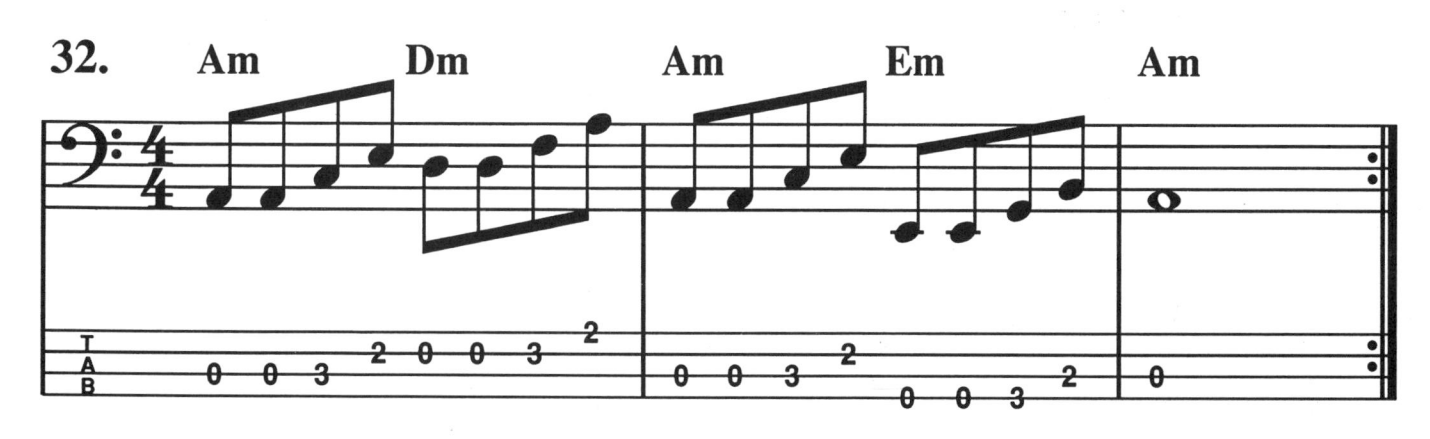

Count   **1 + 2 +** etc.   **1** 2 3 4

New Note on the E String (F)

Fourth string (E string)

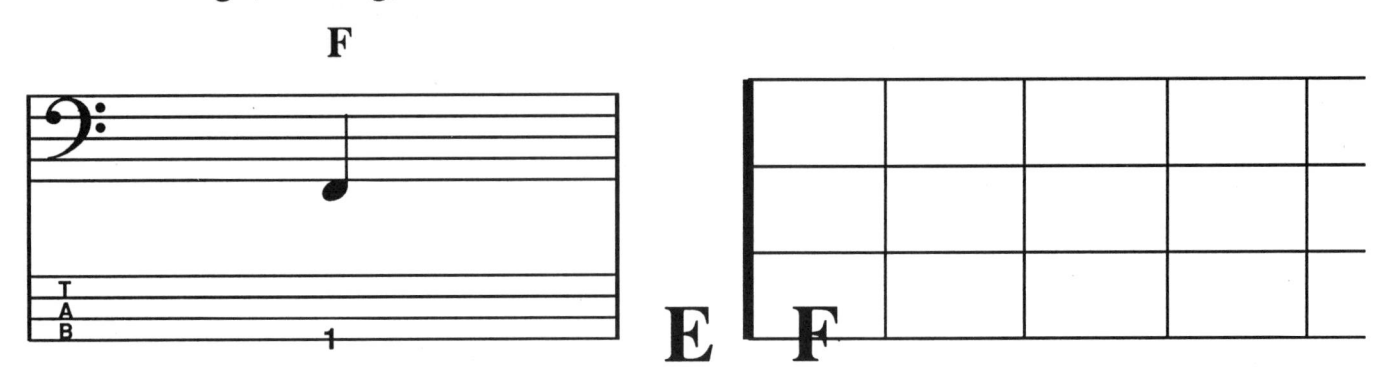

Play the F note with the first finger of your left hand. When playing examples with low F note, your left hand is based around the first four frets as shown in the photo below.

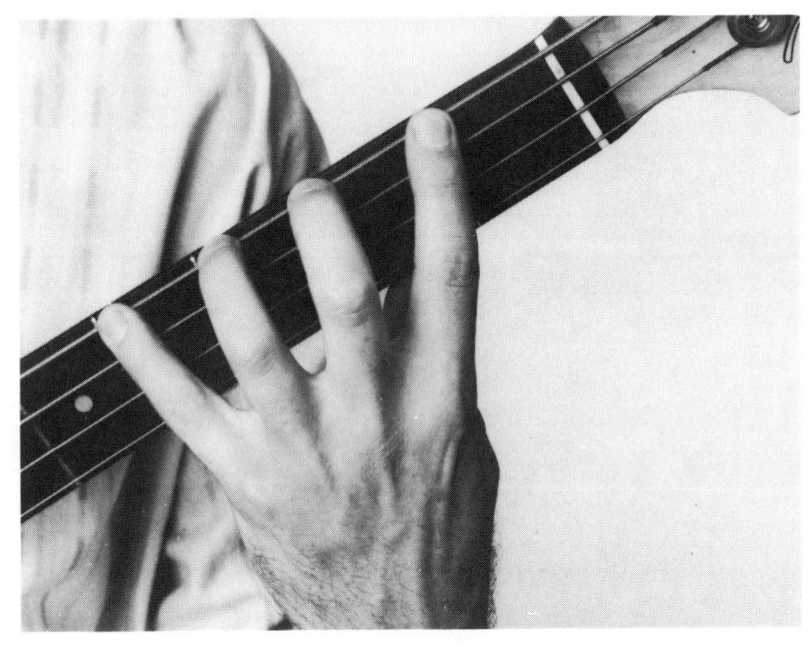

When your left hand is based around the first fret you will need to change your fingering for the other notes as illustrated in Example 33 below.

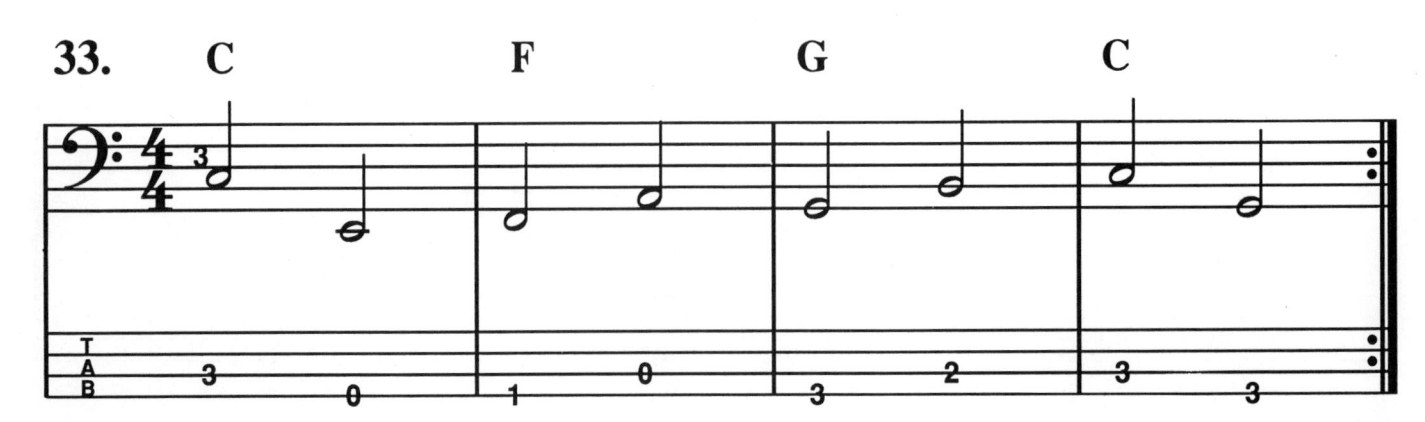

33.

34.

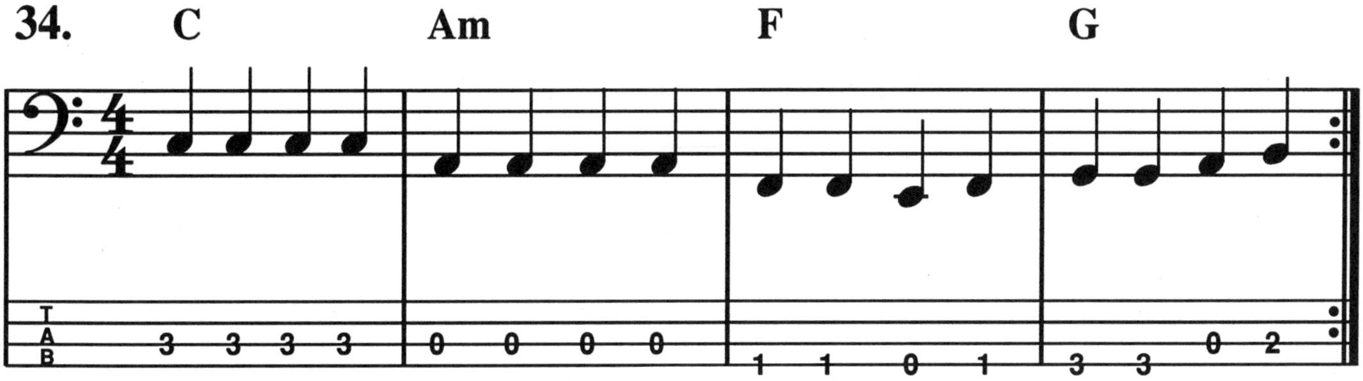

35.

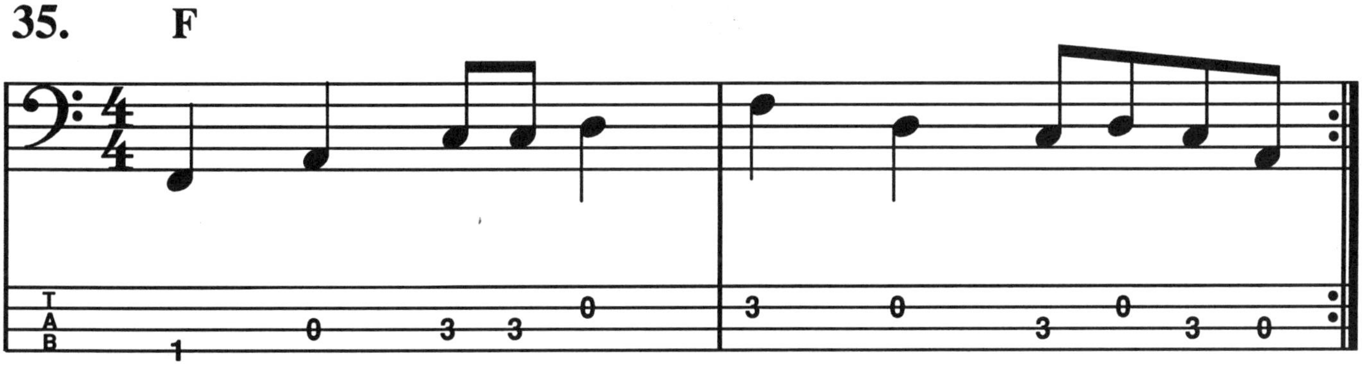

36.

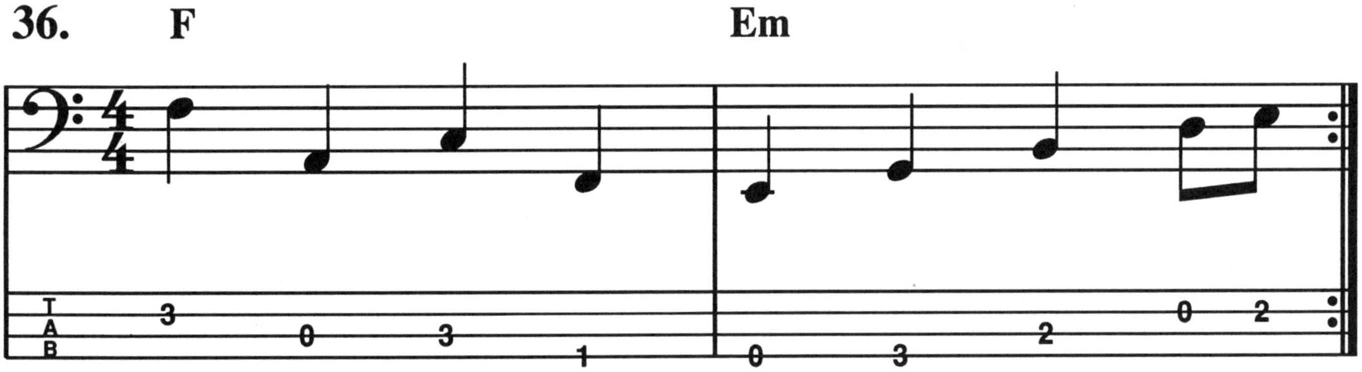

37.

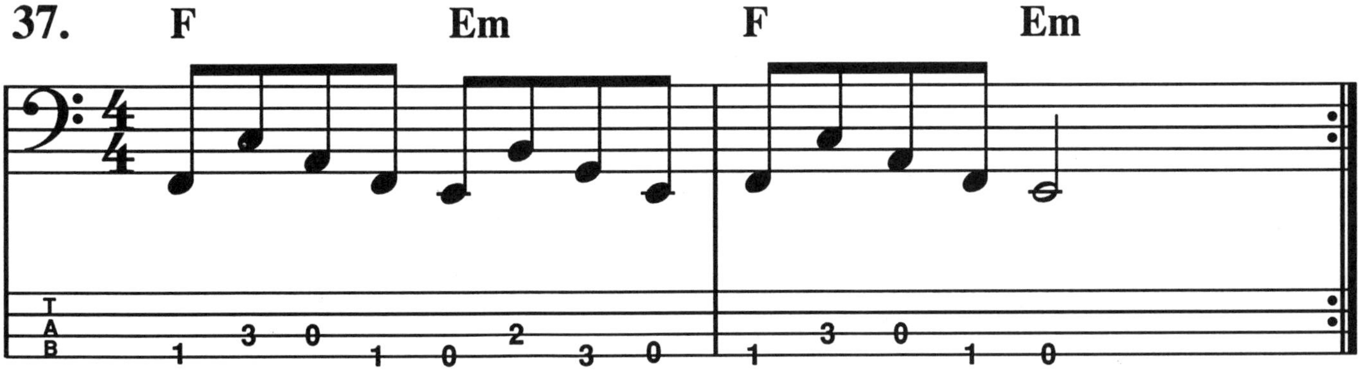

New Notes on the G String (B, C)

First string (G string)

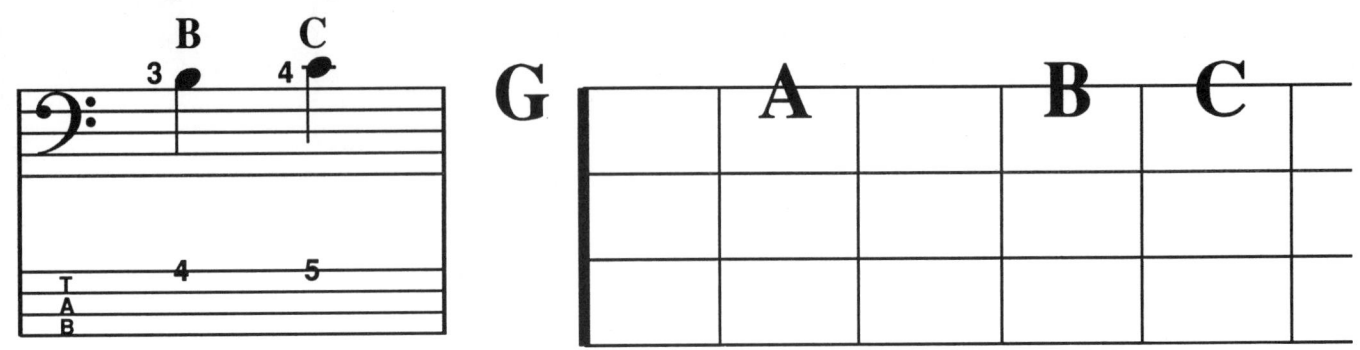

Play the B note with the third finger of your left hand.

Play the C note with the fourth finger of your left hand.

Now that you are using all four fingers to play notes, make sure you have one fret spacing between each finger as shown in the photo below.

Remember to place each finger directly behind the fret to avoid buzzing and to create the best possible sound.

Example 38 uses all the G and D string notes you have learnt.

38.

The Major Scale

The major scale is a series of eight notes in alphabetical order that has the familiar sound

| Do | Re | Mi | Fa | So | La | Ti | Do |

The name of the major scale is taken from its first note (root note).

You now know enough notes to play the C major scale.

Do	Re	Mi	Fa	So	La	Ti	Do
C	D	E	F	G	A	B	C

└ Third String ┘ └ Second String ┘ └──── 1st String ────┘

| Fret | 3 | 0 | 2 | 3 | 0 | 2 | 4 | 5 |
| Finger | 2 | 0 | 1 | 2 | 0 | 1 | 3 | 4 |

The notes of the C major scale have the following pattern on the fretboard.

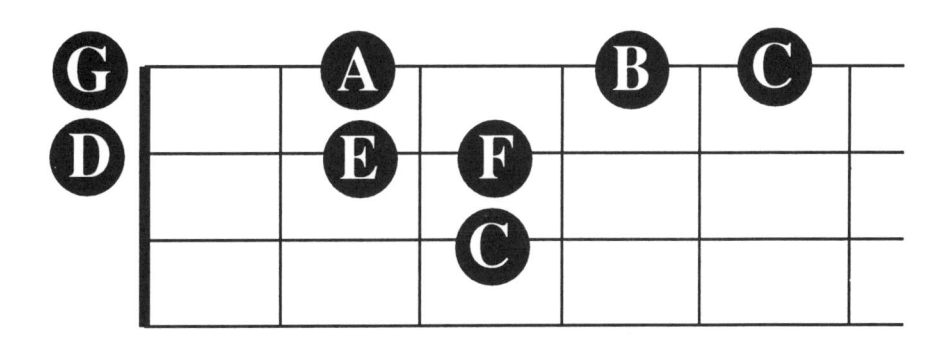

The C major scale over one octave is notated as follows:

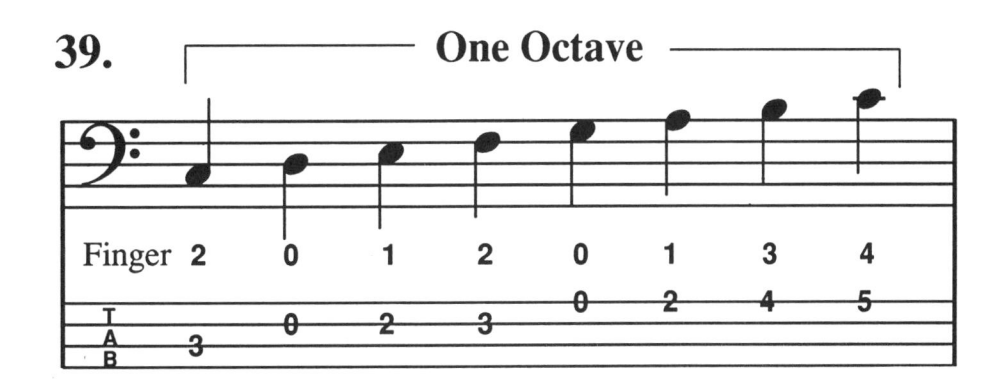

39. ── One Octave ──

Finger 2 0 1 2 0 1 3 4

The Octave

An **octave** is the range of eight notes of a **major scale**. The **first** note and the **last** note of a major scale always have the same name. In the C major scale the distance from lowest C to the C note above it is one octave (eight notes).

Practice playing this scale ascending and descending as a warm up before practice.

Many bass runs and licks are based upon scales.

The bass run in the example below uses all the notes from the C major scale.

40.

The distance of two frets is called a tone.

The distance of one fret is called a semi-tone.

The notes B and C are separated by one semi-tone (1 fret).

The notes E and F are separated by one semi-tone (1 fret).

All other notes are separated by one tone (2 frets).

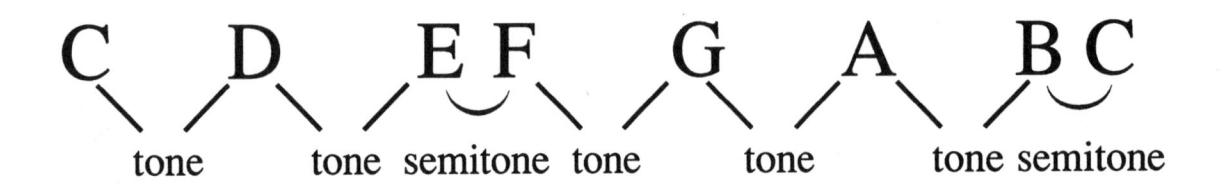

C   D   E F   G   A   B C
 tone   tone semitone tone   tone   tone semitone

Summary of all the notes studied so far.

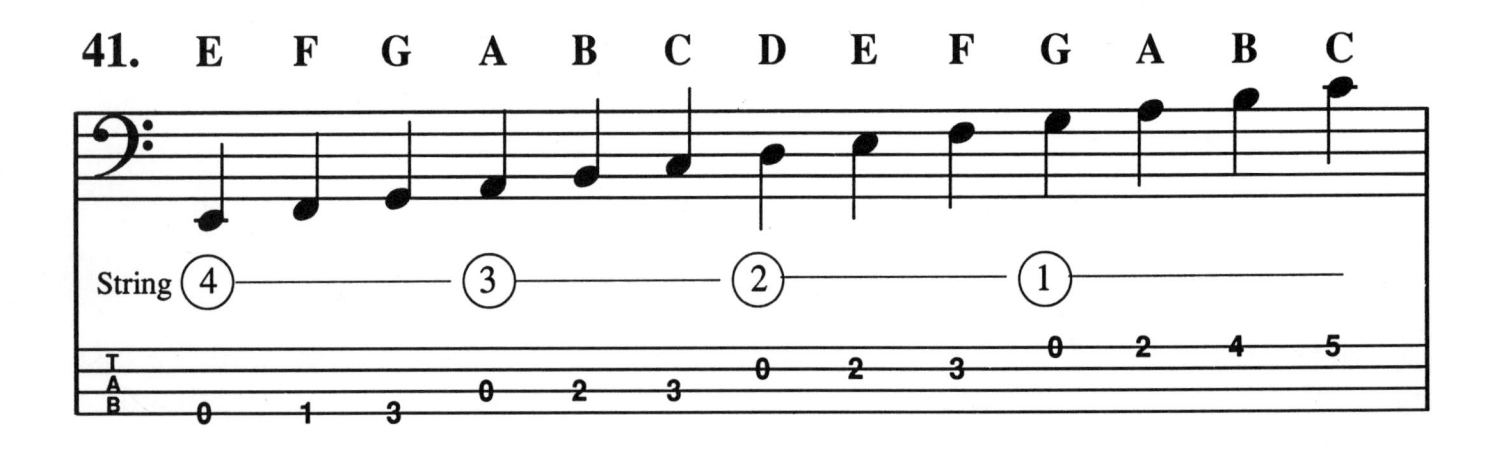

41.   E   F   G   A   B   C   D   E   F   G   A   B   C

Chromatic Scale, Sharps (♯) and Flats (♭)

The chromatic scale is a series of notes that are separated by one semi-tone (i.e. 1 fret).

$$C \quad {}^{C\sharp}_{D\flat} \quad D \quad {}^{D\sharp}_{E\flat} \quad E \quad F \quad {}^{F\sharp}_{G\flat} \quad G \quad {}^{G\sharp}_{A\flat} \quad A \quad {}^{A\sharp}_{B\flat} \quad B \quad C$$

The new notes in between are called sharps and flats.

♯ indicates a sharp, which raises the note by one semitone (1 fret).

♭ indicates a flat which lowers the note by one semitone (1 fret).

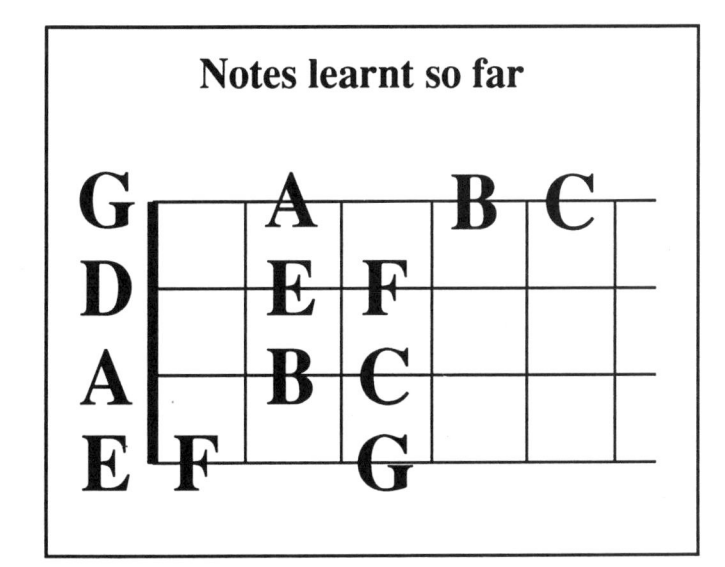

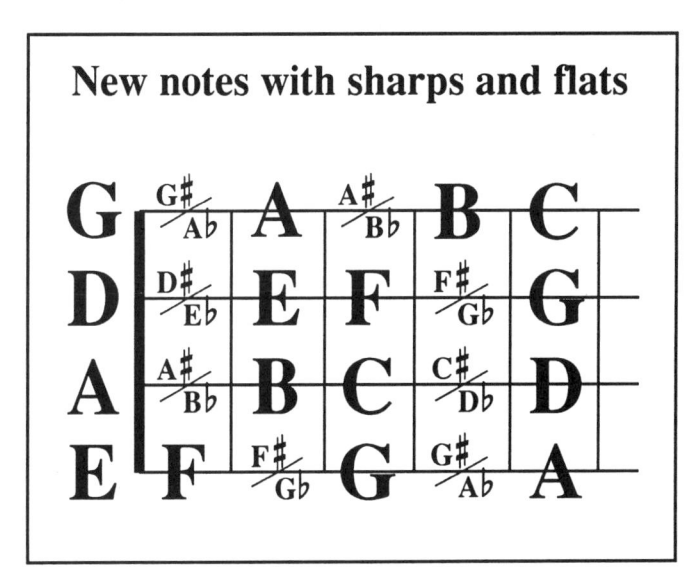

Notes learnt so far	New notes with sharps and flats

The 5th fret of the E string (A note) is the same note as the open A string.

The 5th fret of the A string (D note) is the same note as the open D string.

The 5th fret of the D string (G note) is the same note as the open G string.

These note positions are important to remember because they are the basis for tuning your bass guitar to itself. (See Appendix).

When a sharp or flat note is written on a music stave the symbol (♯ or ♭) is placed before the note.

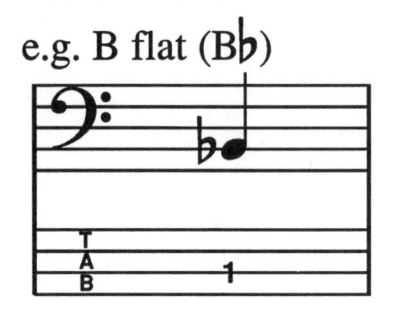

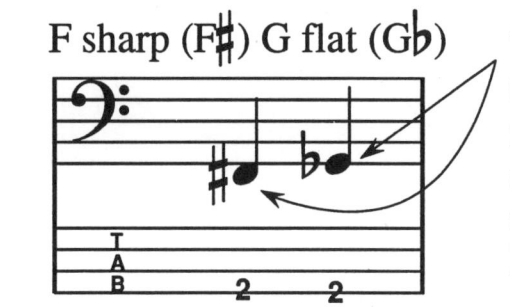

e.g. B flat (B♭)

F sharp (F♯) G flat (G♭)

These two notes have the same position on the fretboard but have different names. In the examples below both F♯ and G♭ are used.

In this example both F notes are sharpened. This is because of the rule that a sharp (or flat), when placed before a note, affects the same note if it reoccurs in the remainder of that bar. Play this example based around the second fret.

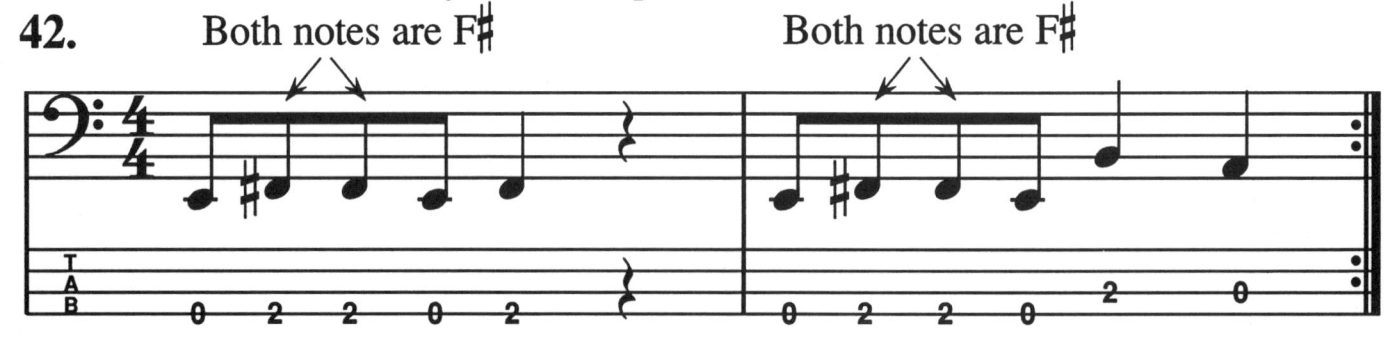

42. Both notes are F♯   Both notes are F♯

Lick 43 is based around the first fret. In bar 9 the G♭ note on the second fret of the E string is used.

43.

Staccato

All the licks you have played so far have been played smoothly (called legato). Another way of playing notes is called staccato. In staccato playing the notes are played short and separate. This is indicated by a dot placed above or below the note e.g.

In the lick below to make the notes staccato, release the pressure on the fretted note (to stop it sounding) immediately after playing it.

The left hand maintains contact with the string at all times.

44.

Riffs

Bass guitarists often use a technique of playing "riffs" against a chord progression. A riff is a pattern of notes that is repeated throughout a progression (or song).

For ease of playing, use the 1st and 3rd fingers as indicated, and when changing from E to F♯ leave the first finger down in preparation for the next E note. This riff can be applied to a 12 bar blues in A. Be sure to observe the rule on page 34, (Ex. 42) for playing sharps in each bar.

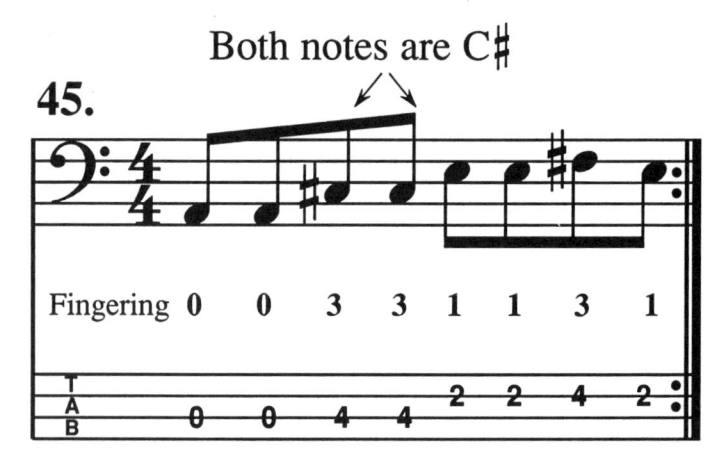

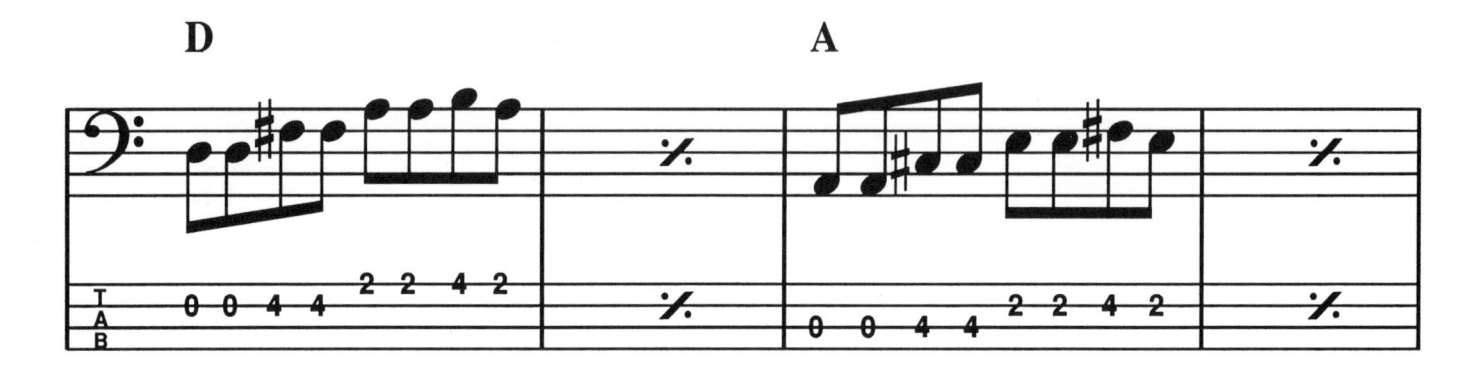

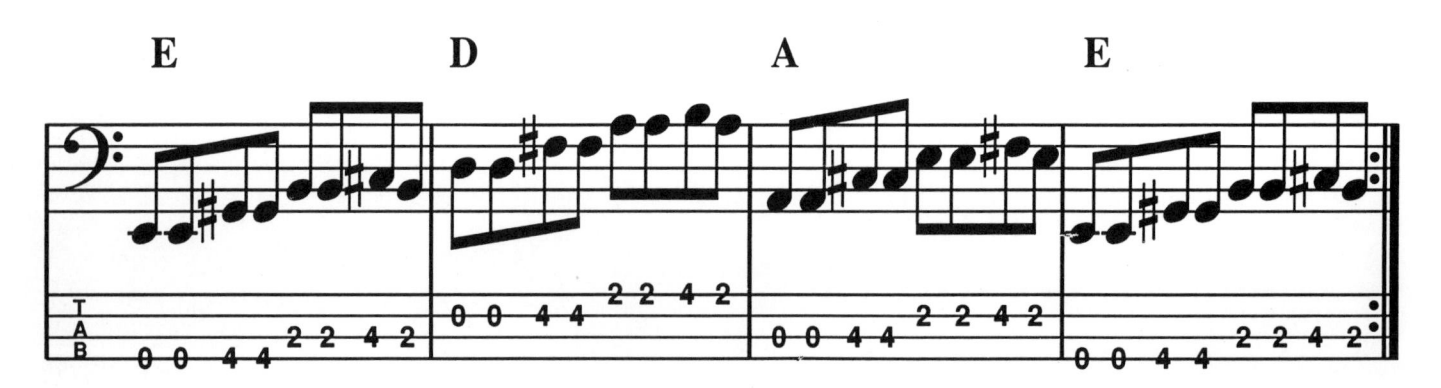

45. Both notes are C♯

46.

You have probably heard this riff style of playing before. Play some records (fifties rock and roll or blues songs would be best) and listen to the bass guitarist.

Chords and Arpeggios

A chord is a group of three or more notes played together. Chords are commonly played by guitarists and keyboard players etc. On the bass guitar, chords are played one note at a time. This is called an arpeggio. The most important chords to learn are the major chord (e.g. C major) and the minor chord (e.g. D minor). These chords are based upon the major scale. (For more information on arpeggios and chords see Progressive Bass Guitar or Progressive Tapping Technique for Bass Guitar.) C is a shorthand way of writing C major. It applies to all major chords. Dm is a shorthand method of writing D minor. It applies to all minor chords. The examples below are commonly used arpeggios. It is important to memorize these arpeggios as they will become very useful in playing bass. These arpeggios start on the root note (i.e. the name of the chord).

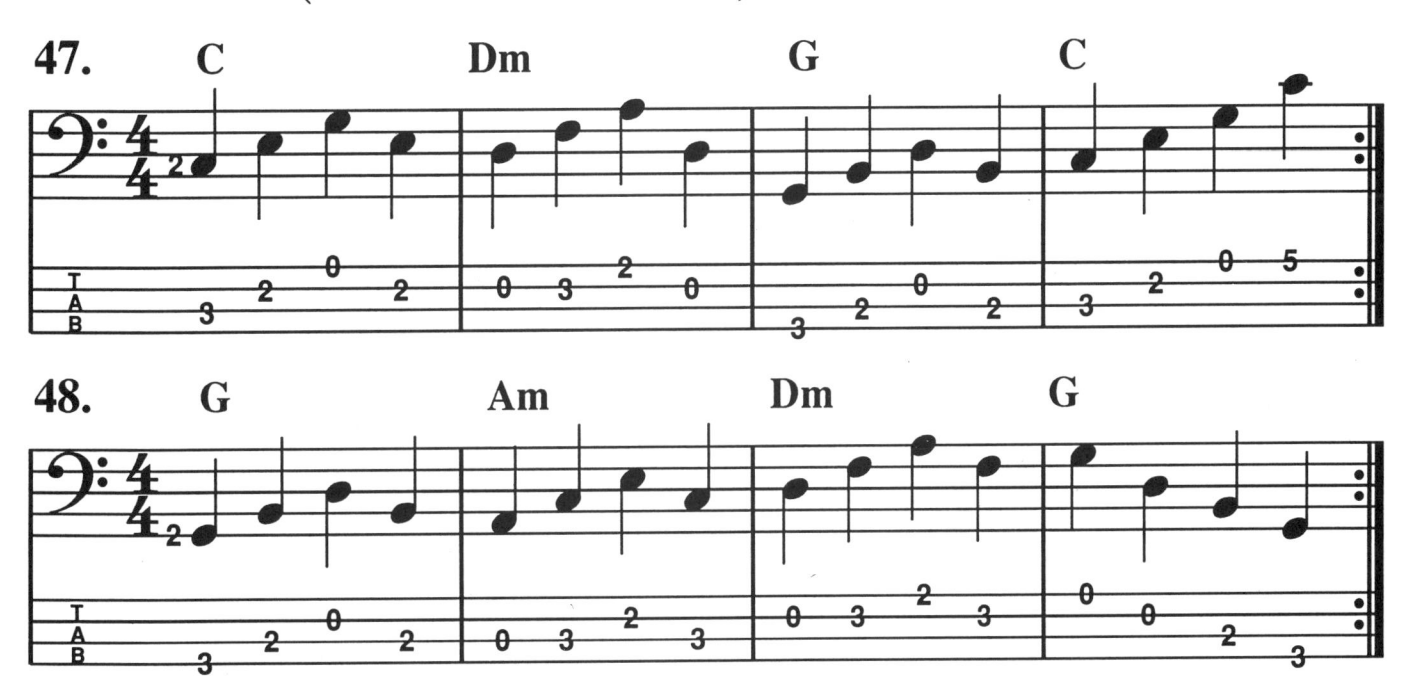

47.

48.

In the two examples below, the F chord arpeggio is played in different octaves.

49.

50.

The notes of an arpeggio can be played in any order. In the example below the arpeggios start on the highest note moving downwards to the root note.

51.

*This chord is called a diminished chord. It is indicated by º after the letter name.

In the next example all open string notes are replaced with fretted notes, which are played with the little finger.

52.

Example 53 uses the same chord progression as Example 49, but this time play the F chord in the lower octave, with the notes of the chord in a different order.

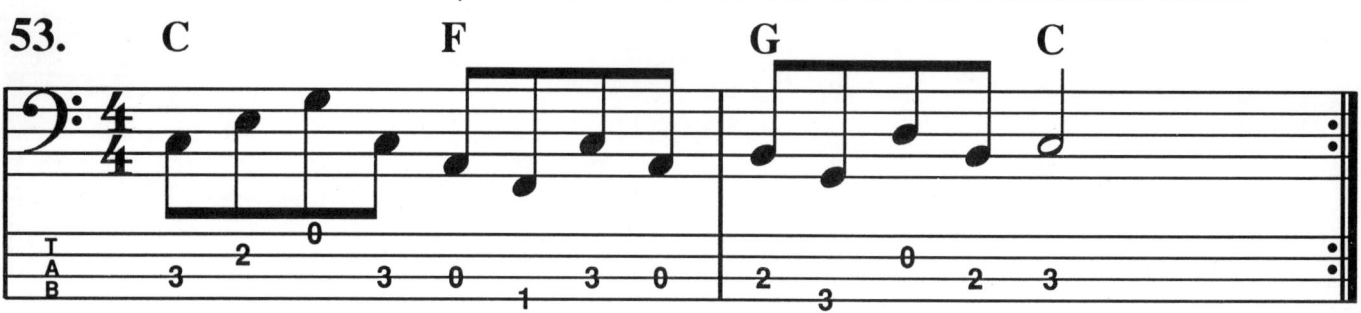

53.

Arpeggio Patterns (major)

The best way of learning arpeggios is to remember the pattern they form on the fretboard. The numbers 2, 1, 4 indicate which left hand finger to use.

Each chord type has its own pattern of notes that can be moved up and down the fretboard or across the strings. The most common pattern for a major chord arpeggio;

C major chord arpeggio pattern

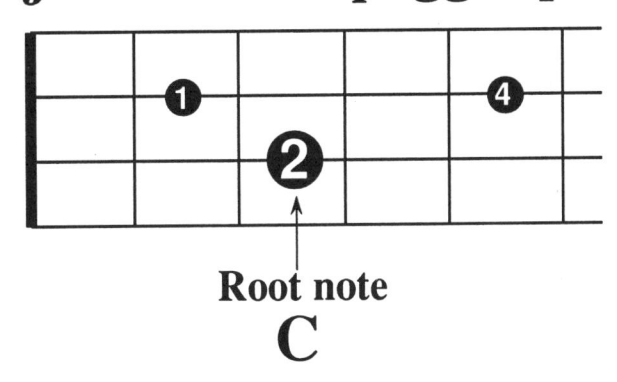

Root note
C

If you play this same pattern starting at the 3rd fret of the second string (D string) the root note will be F. Therefore you are playing an F major chord arpeggio.

F major chord arpeggio pattern

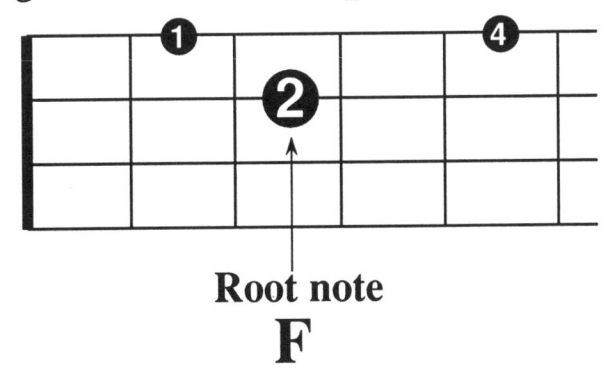

Root note
F

If the F major chord arpeggio is moved up two frets it becomes a G major chord arpeggio.

G major chord arpeggio pattern

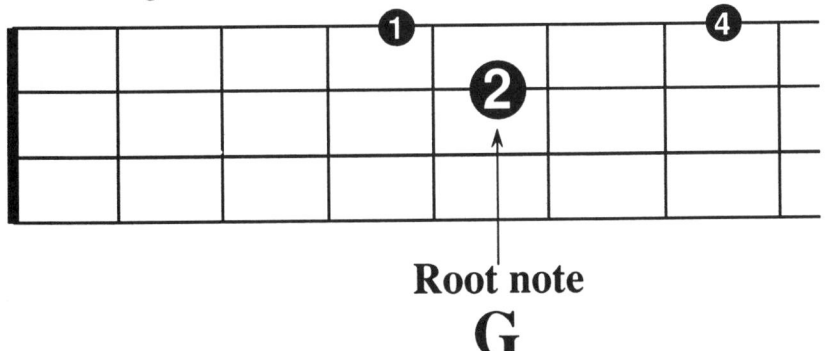

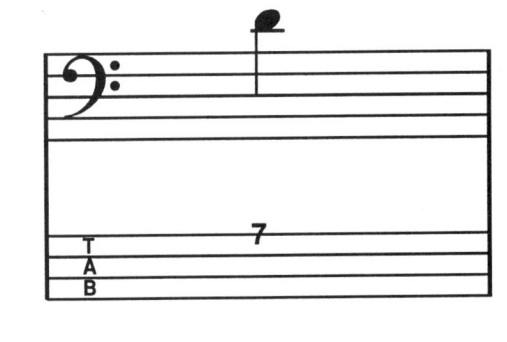

Root note
G

This G major arpeggio introduces a new D note on the 7th fret of the G string.

Shifting Between Chords

It is important to be able to shift between one chord pattern to the next. To practice this, shift between the F and G notes on the D string. Start with the 2nd finger of your left hand on the 3rd fret on the D string (F note) then, without changing the shape of your hand (i.e. don't stretch your fingers) move it until you reach the new note G on the 5th fret of the same string. Have your 2nd finger lightly touching the string when shifting between the notes. Your thumb should also move with your hand. Repeat this movement several times backwards and forwards between the two notes until it feels comfortable and natural.

The example below gives you practice shifting between the F and G arpeggios introduced previously. Note that this example is the same chord progression as Example 53. The G chord this time is played by shifting the F arpeggio up 2 frets.

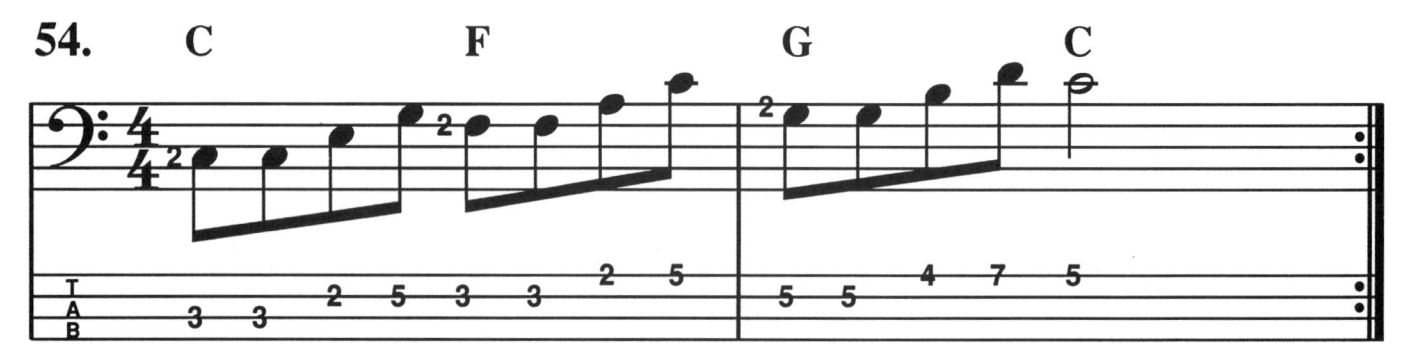

54.

First and Second Endings

The following turnaround progression uses first and second endings. On the first time through the progression, ending one is played (|1.   ), then the progression is repeated (as indicated by the repeat sign), and ending two is played (|2.   ). Be careful not to play both endings together.

55.

The 12 Bar Blues Progression

On page 17 you were introduced to the 12 bar blues progression as outlined below.

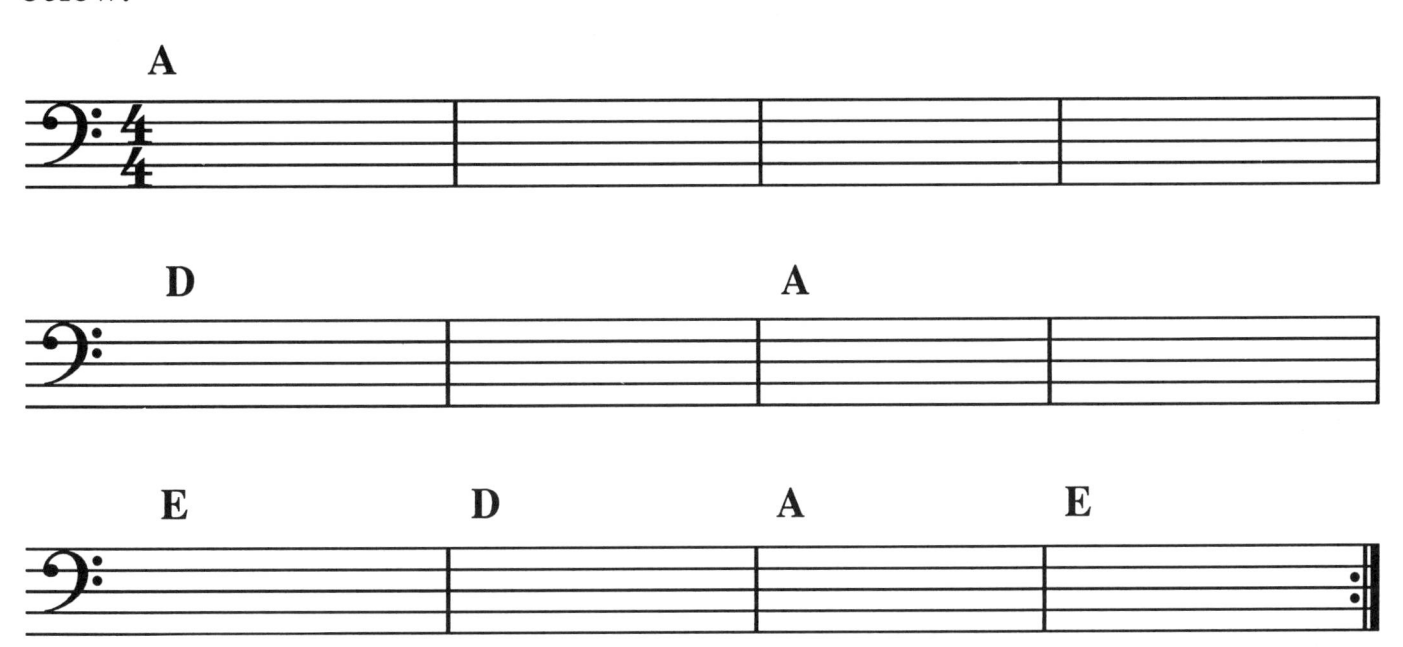

```
     A
𝄢 4/4 |        |        |        |        |

     D                  A
𝄢    |        |        |        |        |

     E        D         A        E
𝄢    |        |        |        |        :||
```

Underneath each chord roman numerals have been written to indicate the basic chords used in 12 bar progressions. It is important for you to remember that 12 bar blues in any key uses the 3 chords, I, IV and V in the following sequence.

```
|| I    |      |      |      |
|  IV   |      |  I   |      |
|  V    |  IV  |  I   |  V   :||
```

For example in the key of C the I, IV and V chords are C, F and G respectively. In the key of G the I, IV and V chords are G, C and D.

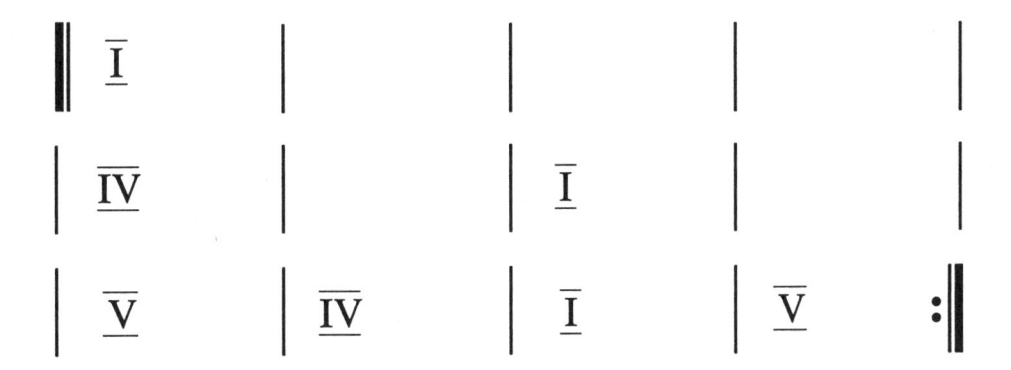

12 Bar in C

```
|| C I  |      |      |      |
|  F IV |      | C I  |      |
|  G V  | F IV | C I  | G V :||
```

12 Bar in G

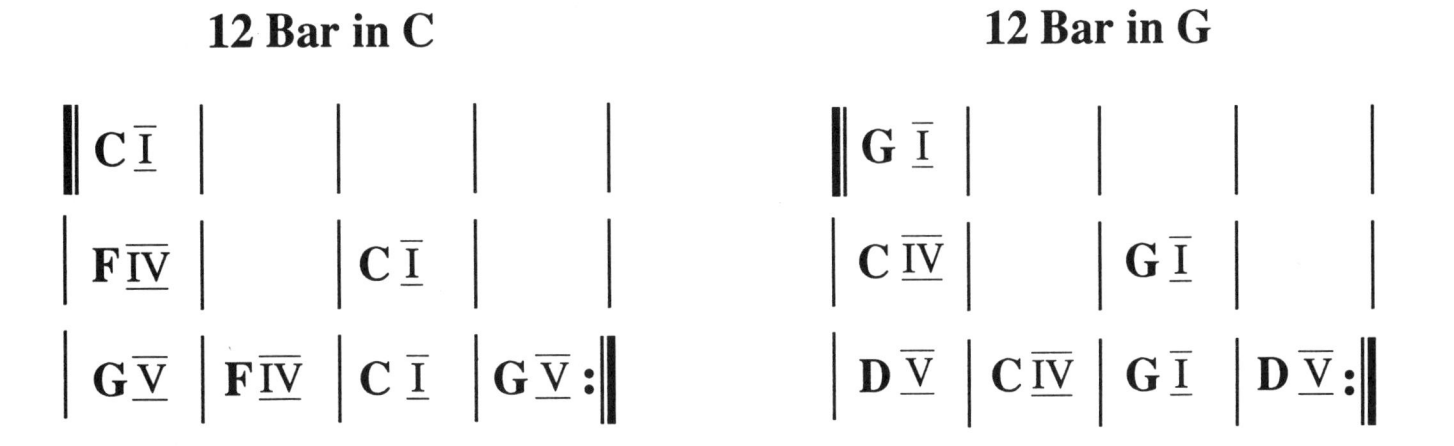

```
|| G I  |      |      |      |
|  C IV |      | G I  |      |
|  D V  | C IV | G I  | D V :||
```

12 Bar Riff

One page 36 you were introduced to the style of playing riffs over a chord progression. The following example, riff 1, is played against the 12 bar blues in the key of A.

Riff 1A
56. A

For each bar of the A chord, riff one starts at the A note on the 5th fret of the 4th string. Play this riff slowly and smoothly, using the correct fingering.

Riff 1B
57. D

When the progression changes to a D chord (bar 5) the riff moves across to the third string, commencing on the D note (5th fret). You will notice that the fingering is still the same and that the basic "shape" of the riff has not altered.

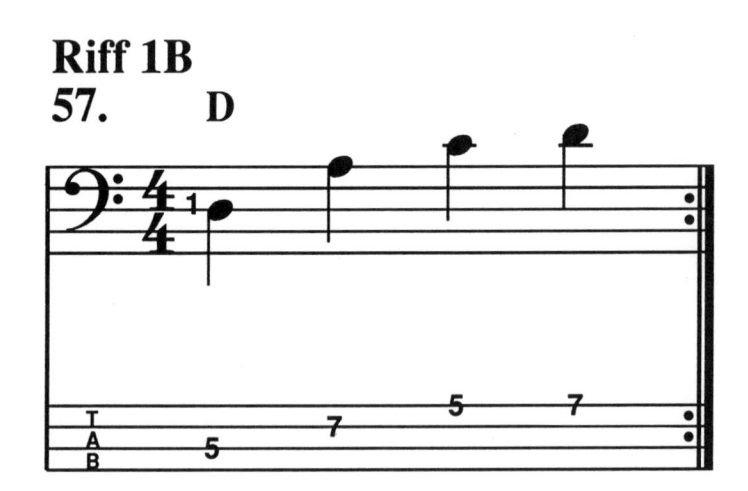

Riff 1C
58. E

For the E chord (bar 9), the riff shape begins on the 3rd string at the 7th fret. Once again, the fingering and basic riff shape remain the same.

Here is the complete 12 bar in A using Riff 1A, B and C.

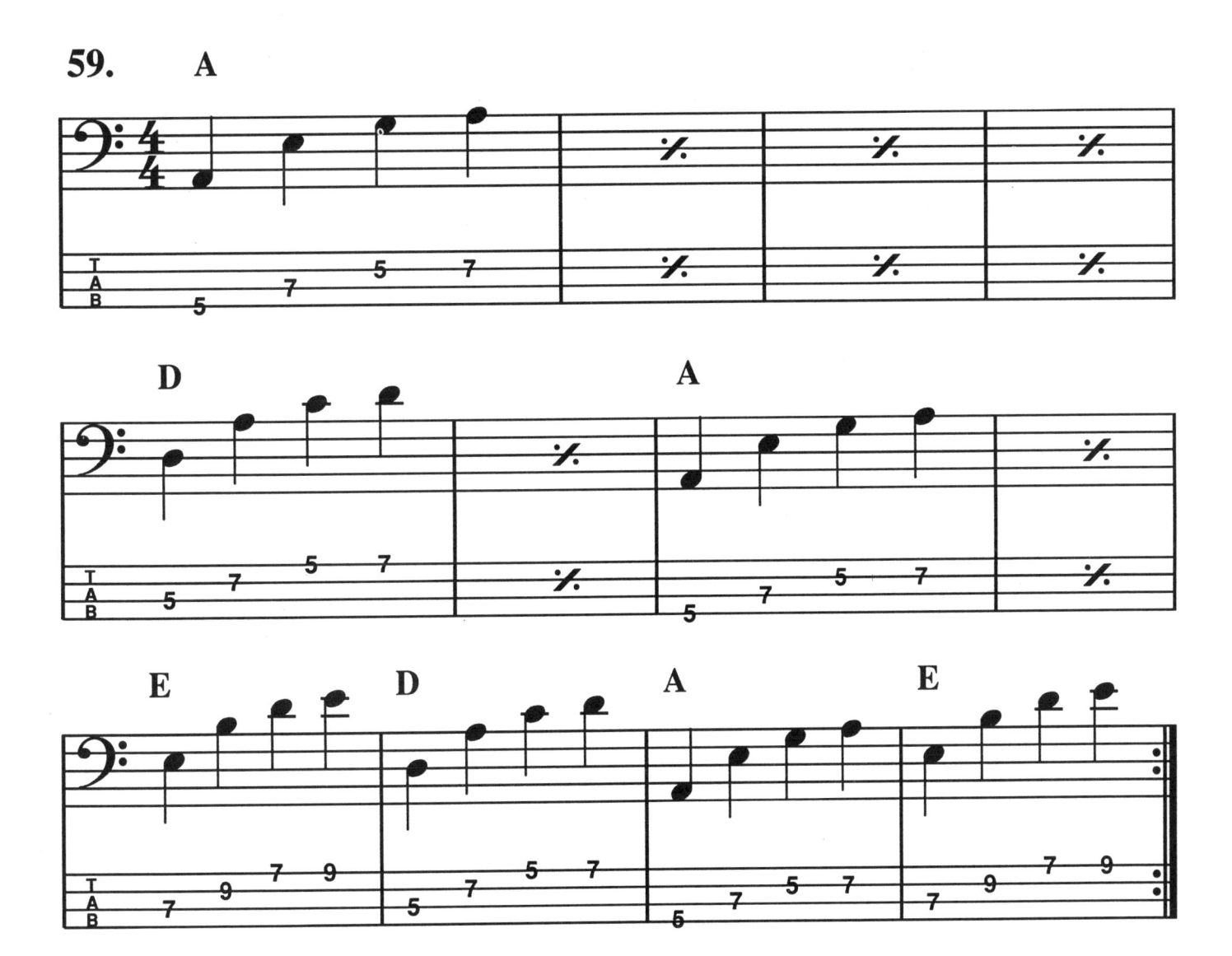

59.

Memorize the above 12 Bar Blues and then transpose it to other keys as outlined on page 41.

Riff Variations

Variations to a basic riff can be achieved by changing the sequence and/or timing of the notes. For example, riff 1 could be varied as such:

60. A

Variation One – altering the note sequence.

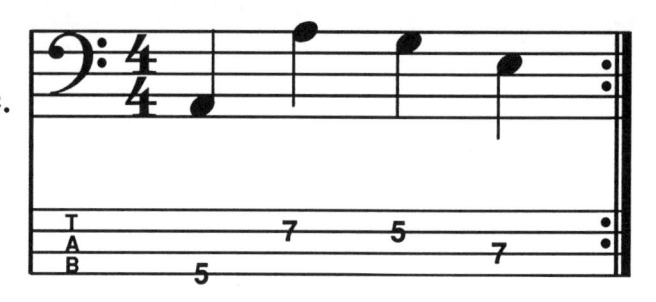

61. A

Variation Two – altering the timing.

Variation Three – altering the sequence and timing.

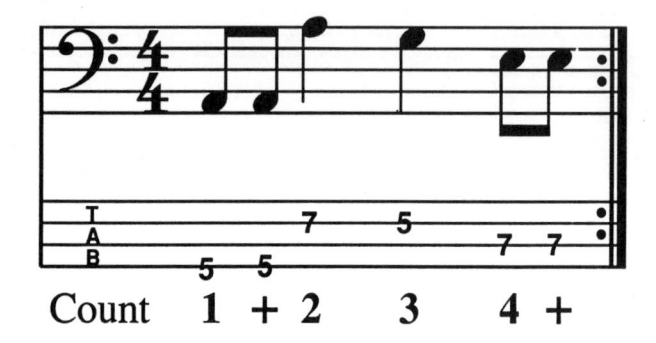

62. A

Count 1 + 2 3 4 +

63. A

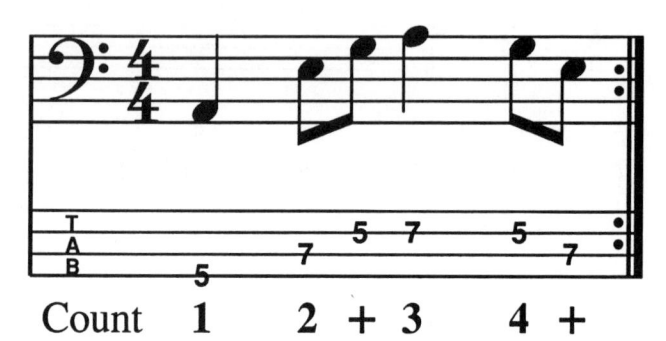

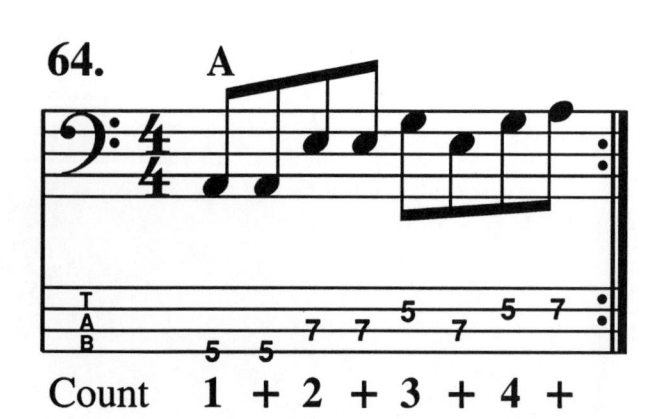

Count 1 2 + 3 4 +

64. A

Count 1 + 2 + 3 + 4 +

Play each of these variations against the 12 bar in A. Experiment with some of your own combinations and transpose them into different keys.

Arpeggio Patterns (minor)

Am chord arpeggio pattern with open A

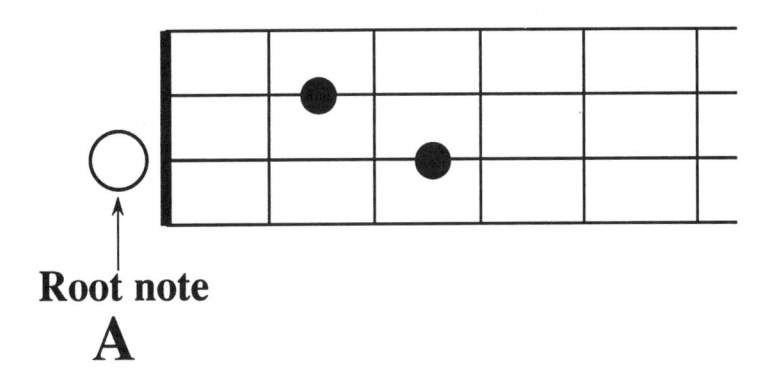

Root note
A

Am arpeggio chord pattern on the 5th fret, no open strings

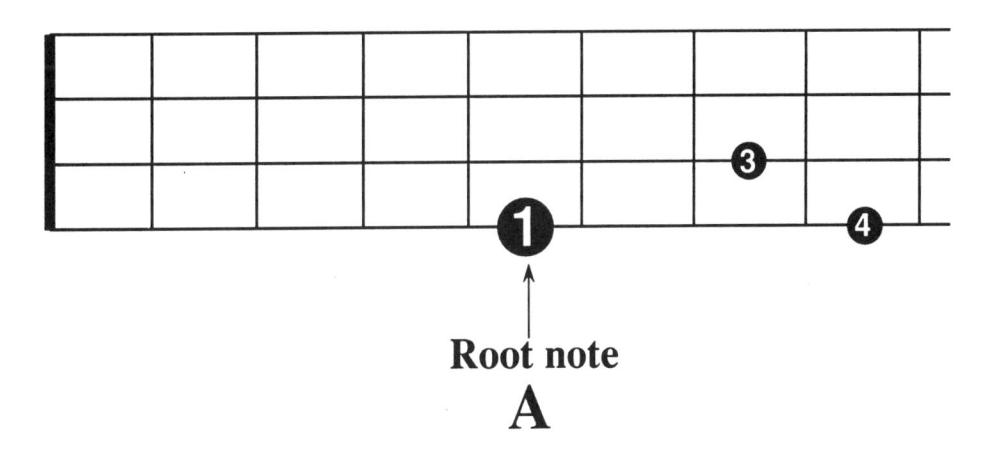

Root note
A

The minor arpeggio chord pattern can be transposed in the same way as the major pattern without changing the shape or fingering. The principal is similar to riff playing where the pattern starts on a different fret or a different string, e.g.

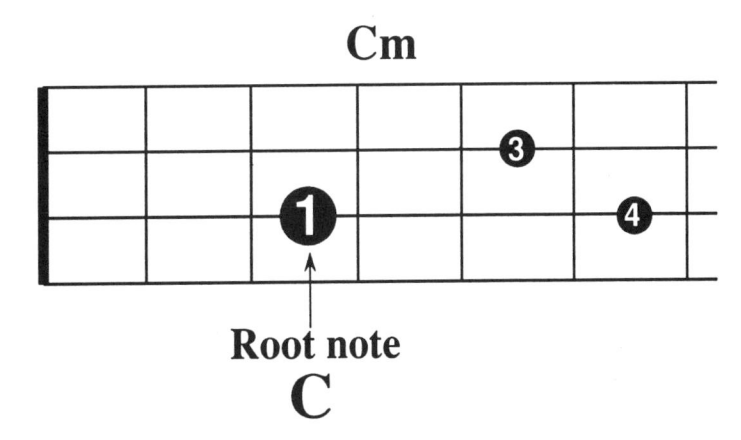

Cm

Root note
C

The Cm arpeggio chord pattern has its root note on the 3rd fret of the A string.

Memorize the shape of the minor arpeggio chord pattern so that you can apply it when it occurs in the music.

Chord Progression

| C | Am | F | G ||

Lick 65 uses only root notes.

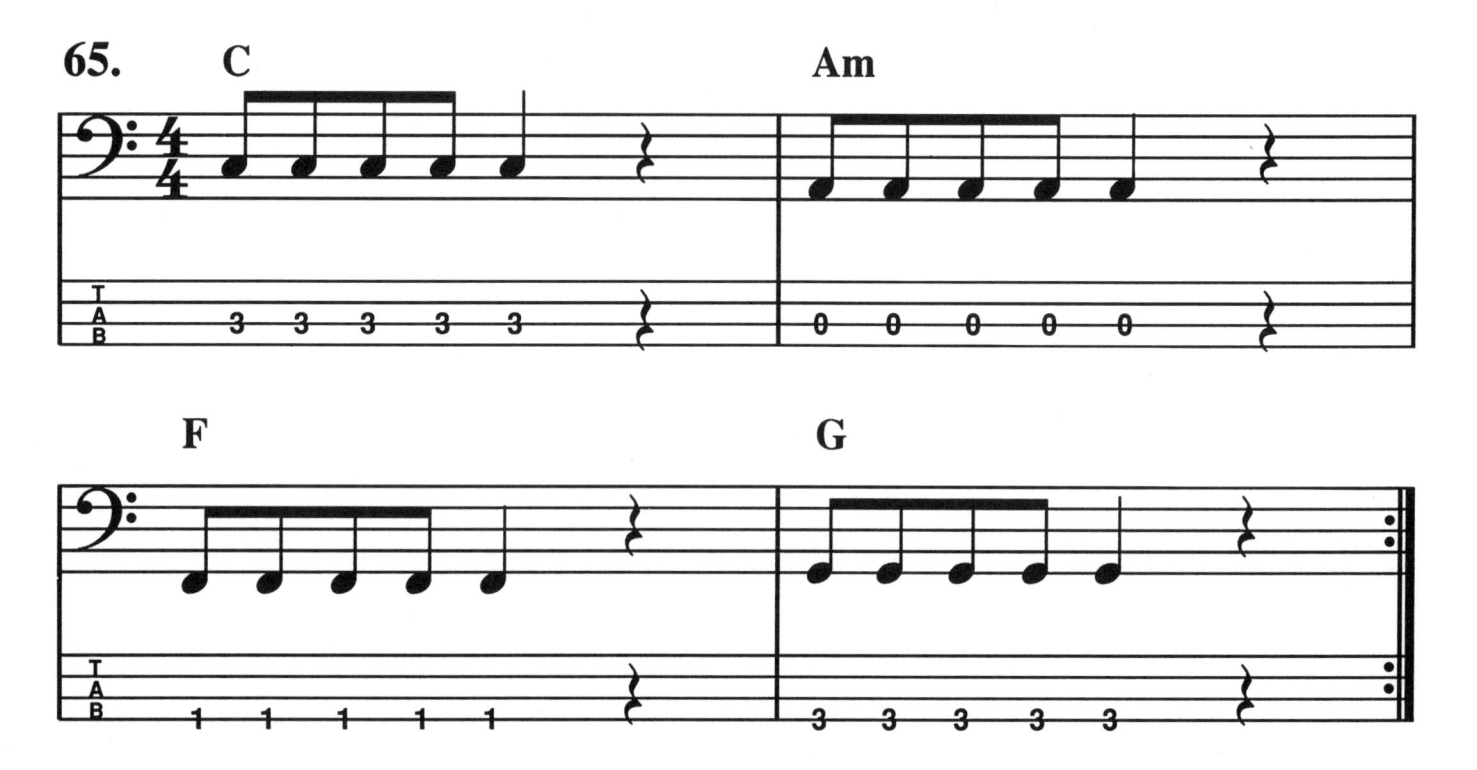

65.

The next two examples use the Am chord with open A string.

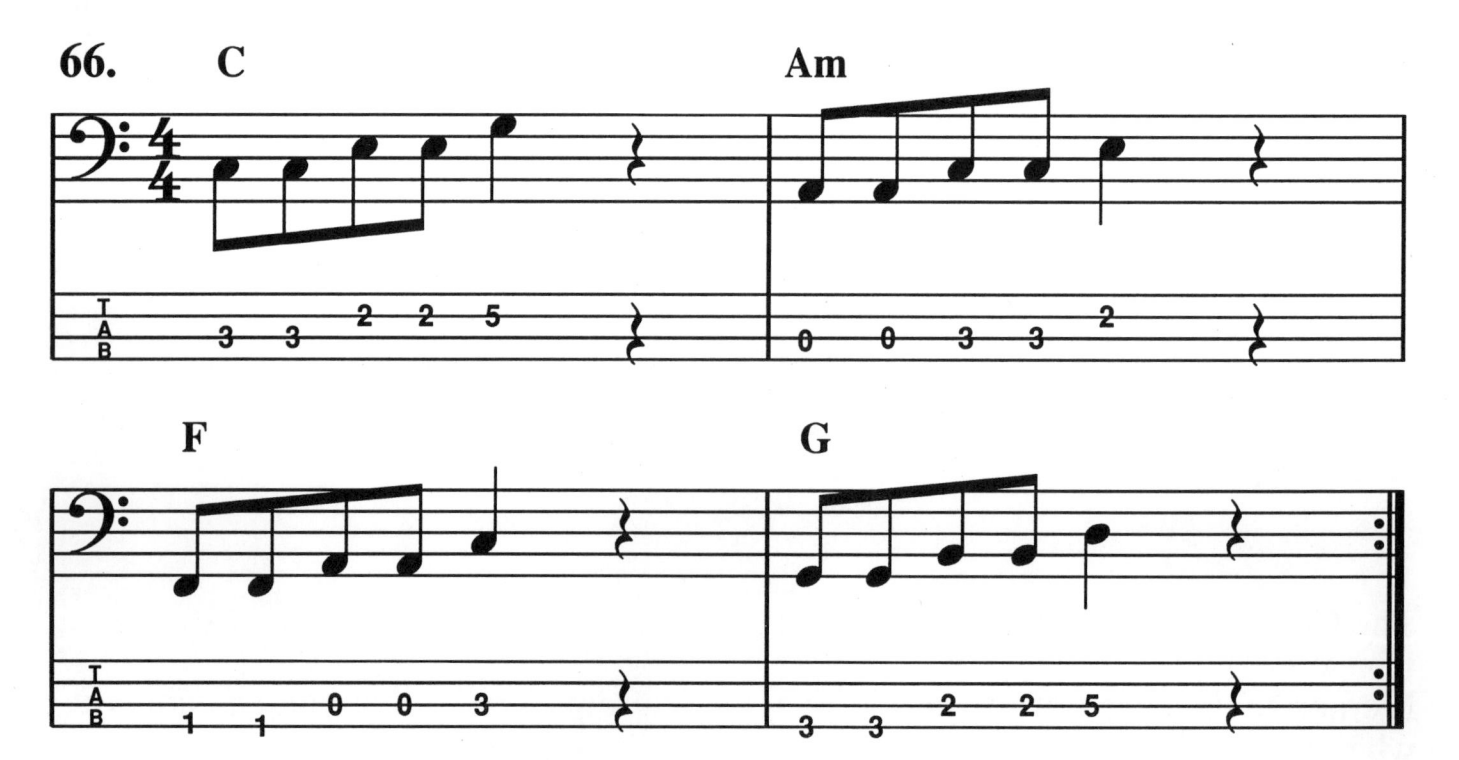

66.

67.

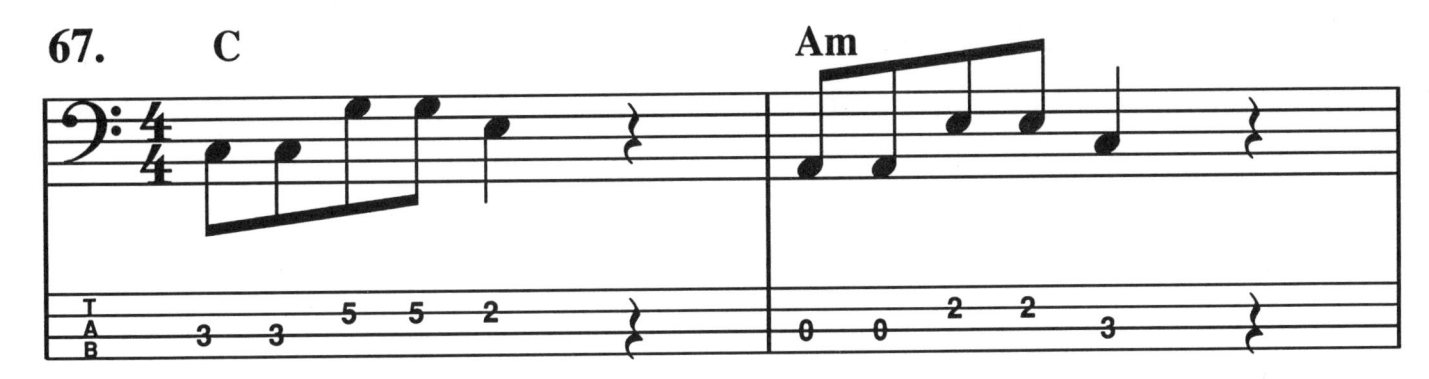

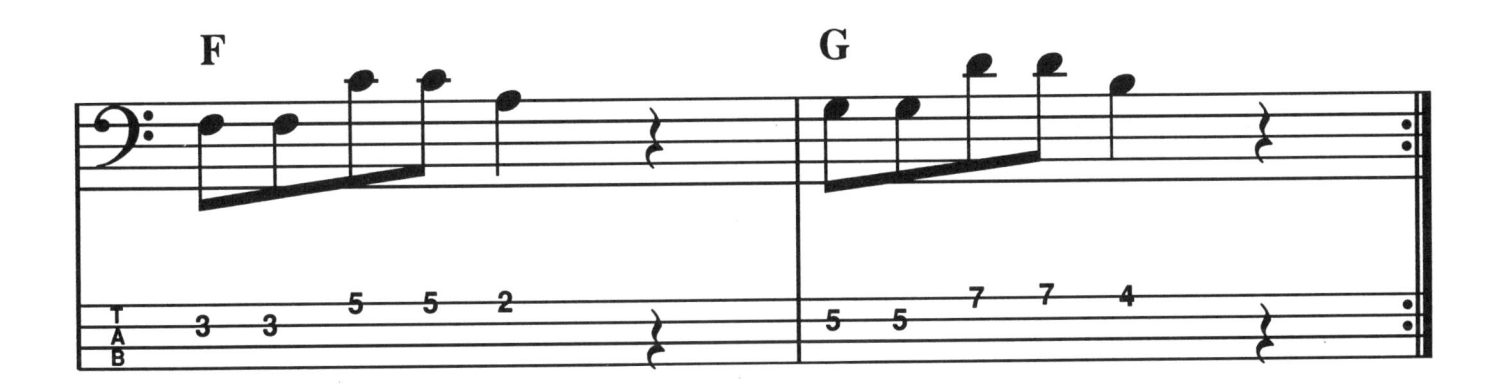

The example below uses the minor chord arpeggio pattern further up the neck (3rd fret) as outlined before (no open strings).

68.

The Dotted Quarter Note

Lick 69 introduced the dotted half note worth 3 counts. The licks below introduce the dotted quarter note which is worth 1½ counts i.e. the dot after the quarter note increases its value by half.

♩ = 1 count   ♩. = 1½ counts

69.

Count 1 2 + 3 4   1 2 + 3 4   etc.

70.

Count 1 2 + 3 4 etc.

71. Riff 2A   **72. Riff 2B**

73. Riff 2C   **74. Riff 2D**

Memorize these riffs and use them on the above chord progression. Make up your own riffs.

The Tie

In music, the tie is a curved line joining two (or more) notes of the same pitch, where the second note(s) is not played, but its time value is added to that of the first note.

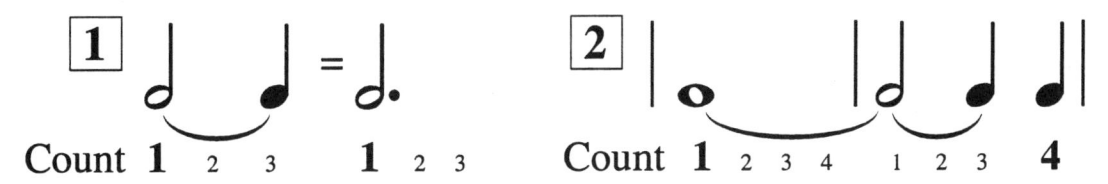

In Example Two, the first note is held for seven counts.

A tie is necessary if a note is played over a bar line, as in Example Two above, and in the 2 bar riff below.

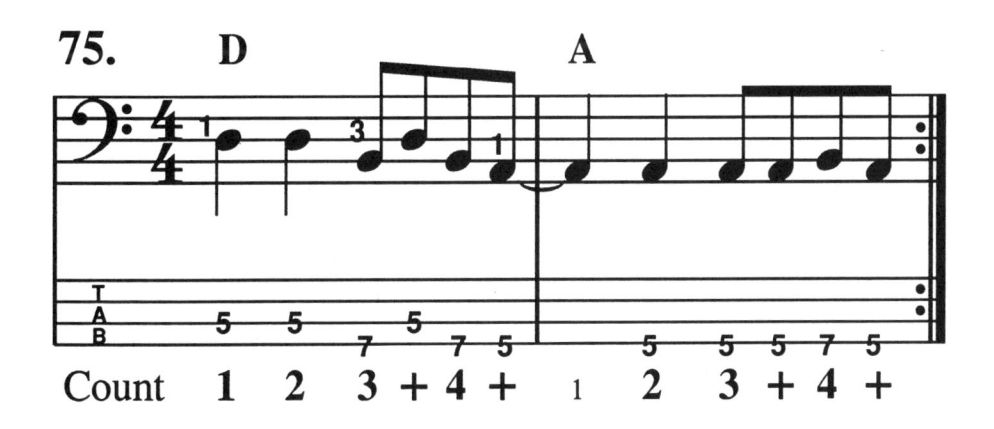

75.

In tablature notation the curved line of a tie is not necessary.

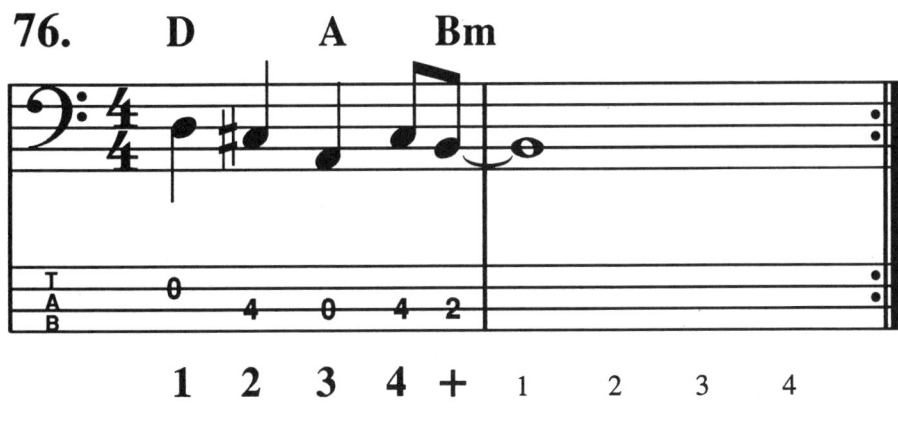

76.

Lick 77 uses a tie within the bar.

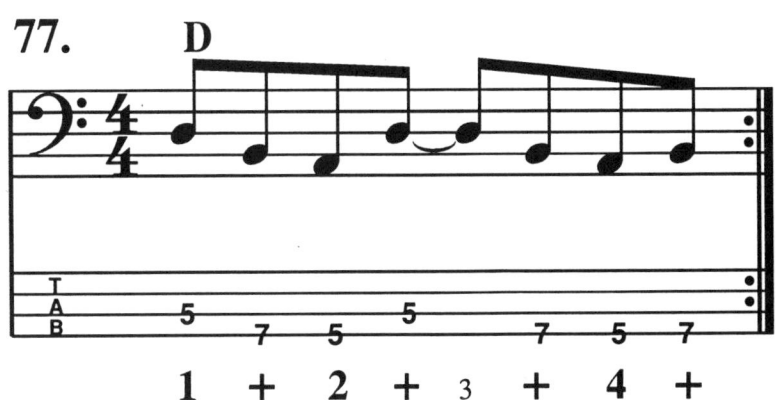

77.

Eighth Note Rest

A staccato feel can be created in the previous lick by using an eighth note rest, 𝄾, on the 3rd beat. The eighth note rest indicates half a beat of silence, which, in the above example occurs on the 3rd beat. The rest is achieved by releasing pressure on the left hand.

78.

Count   1 + 2 + 3 + 4 +

In the two bar lick below the eighth note rest is used on the first count of the second bar.

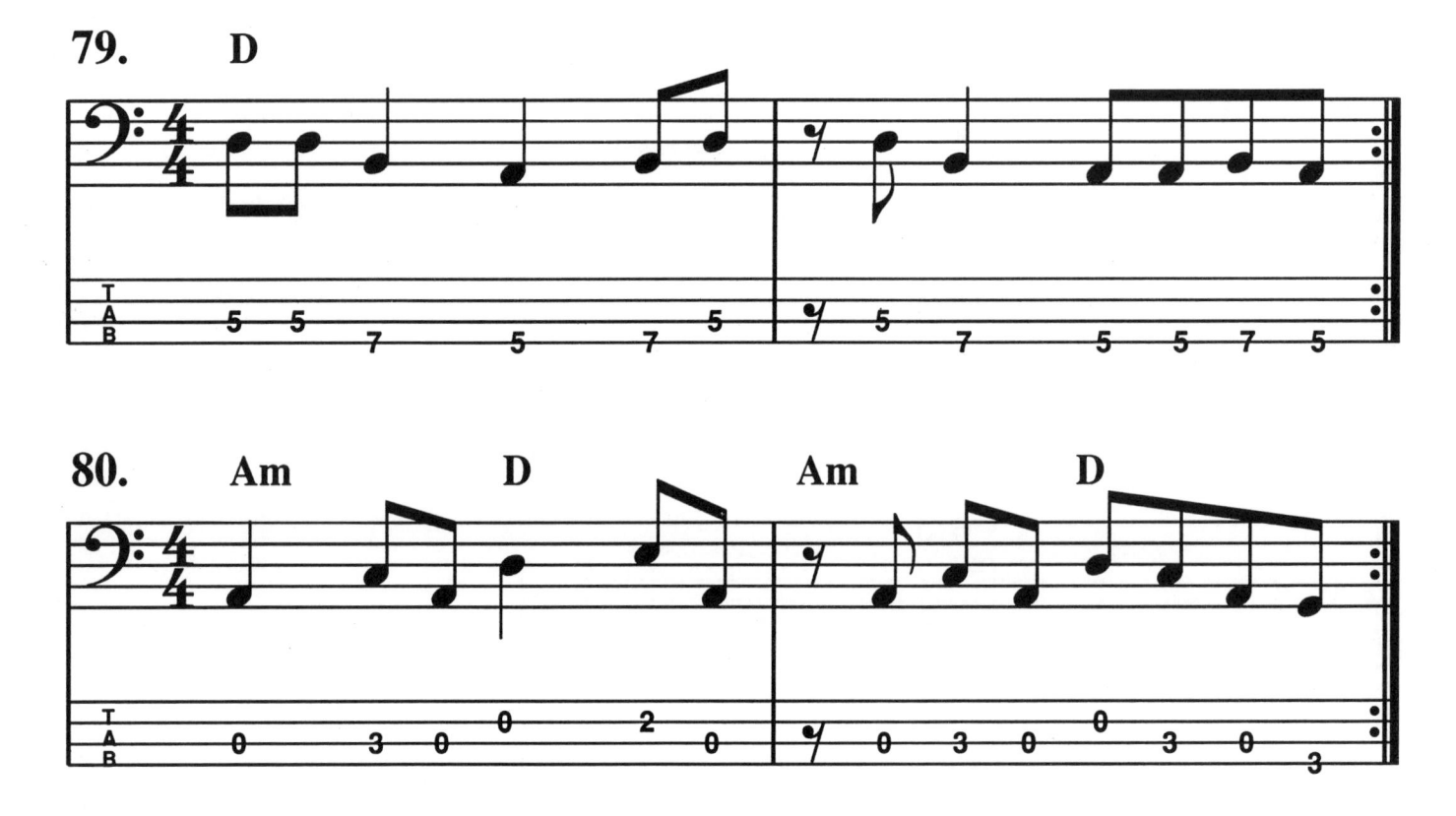

79.

80.

Here is another two bar riff combining the 8th note rest and a tie.

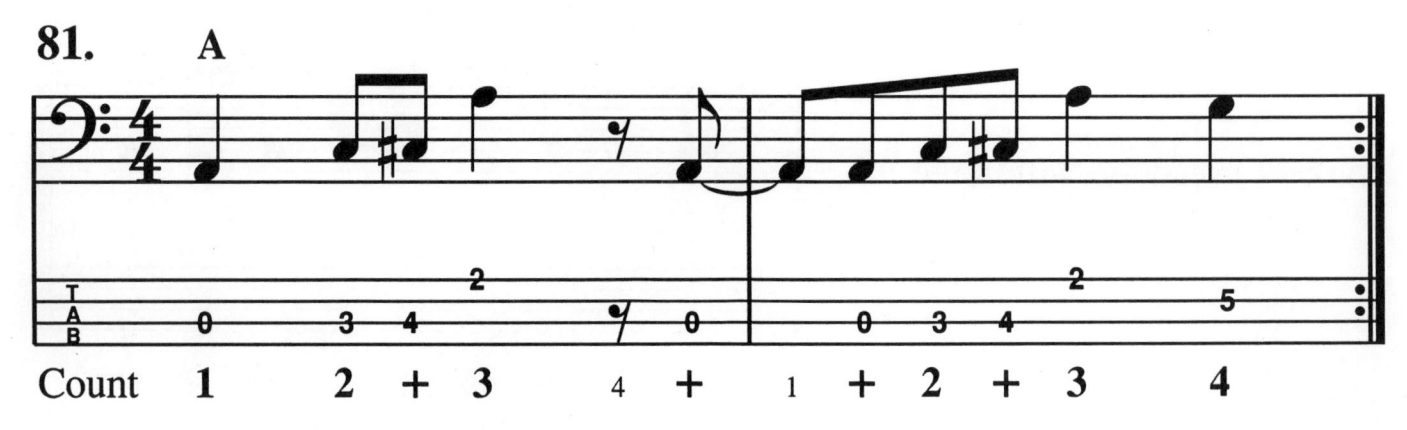

81.

Count   1   2 + 3   4 +   1 + 2 + 3   4

Lead In

Lick 82 involves the use of lead-in (or pick-up) notes which are notes that are played before the first bar of music. The lick commences on the second half of the third beat.

82.

Count   + 4 +   1   2 + 3 + 4 +   1   2   3 + 4 +

Natural (♮)

A natural ♮ is used to cancel out the effect of a sharp or flat.

The example below uses a B flat in the lead in followed by a B natural. Remember to play the two C notes in the first bar with a staccato feel (see p35).

83.

Syncopation

Syncopation can be defined as the placing of an accent on a normally unaccented beat, e.g. in 4/4 time the normal accent is on the first and third beats:

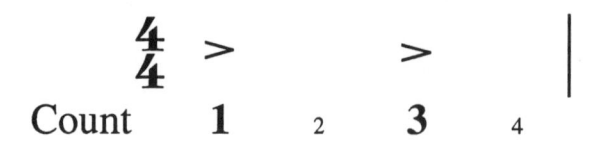

so examples of syncopation could be:

The accent can be achieved by merely playing louder, or by the use of ties, rests and staccato notes. The previous licks have been examples of syncopation.

The following licks use octave notes. The accent has been placed on the "and" count of each beat and syncopation is highlighted by the use of eighth note rests.

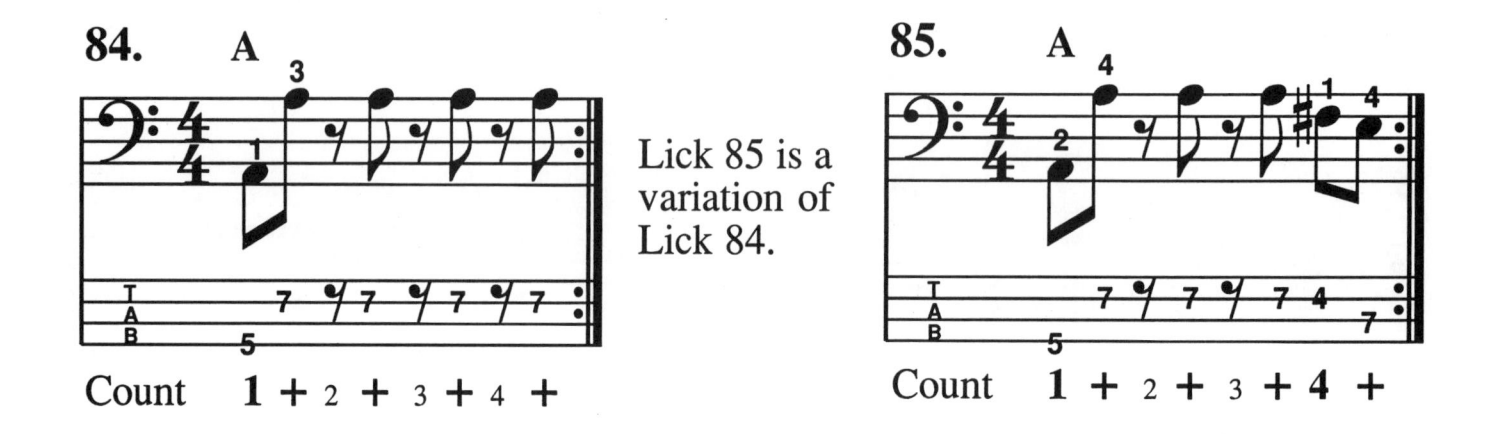

84.

Count 1 + 2 + 3 + 4 +

Lick 85 is a variation of Lick 84.

85.

Count 1 + 2 + 3 + 4 +

The timing of the following lick is the same as that of Lick 84, but the syncopation is achieved by the use of ties, creating a smooth feel.

86.

Count 1 + 2 + 3 + 4 +

Example 87 uses ties to create a smooth syncopated feel.

87.

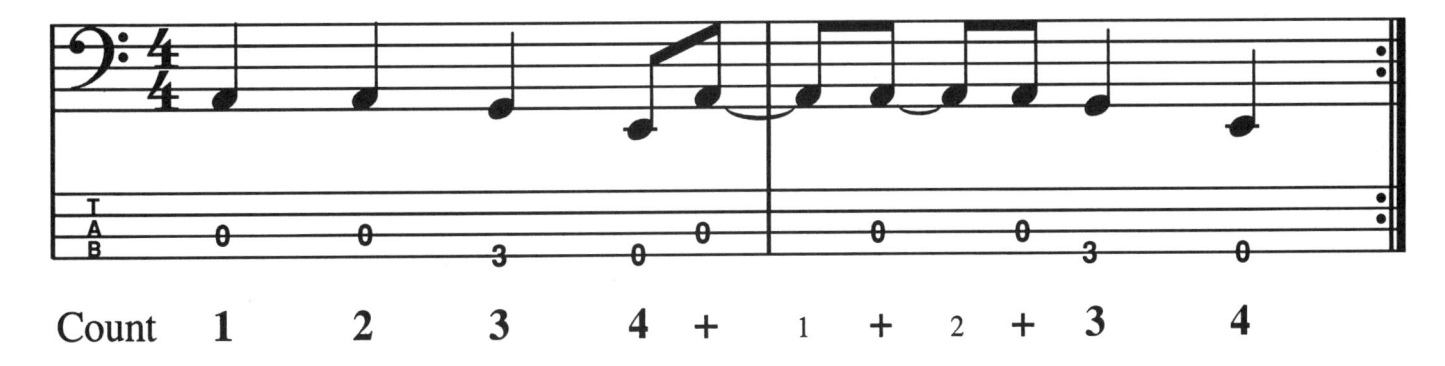

Count   1   2   3   4 +   1 + 2 + 3   4

The next three examples all use a syncopated feel with staccato.

88.

Count   1   2 + 3 + 4 +   1   2 + 3 + 4 +

89.

Count   1 + 2 + 3 + 4 +   1 + 2 + 3   4

90.

Count   1   2   3   4 +   1 + 2 + 3   4

Eighth Note Triplets

In triplet timing, three evenly spaced notes are played in each beat (indicated thus ♪♪♪).

They should be played with an accent on the first note of each group of three (i.e. accent each note that falls "on" the beat).

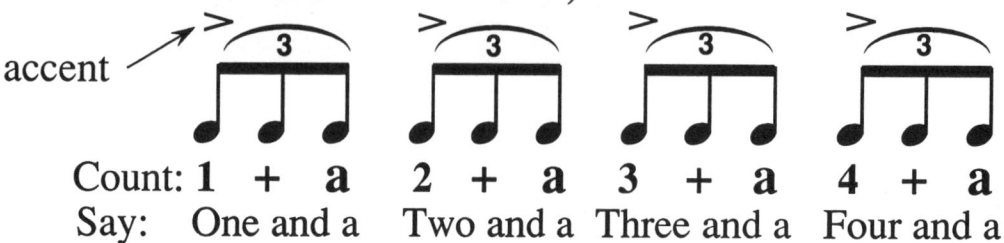

accent

Count: 1 + a   2 + a   3 + a   4 + a
Say: One and a Two and a Three and a Four and a

The following lick uses triplets.

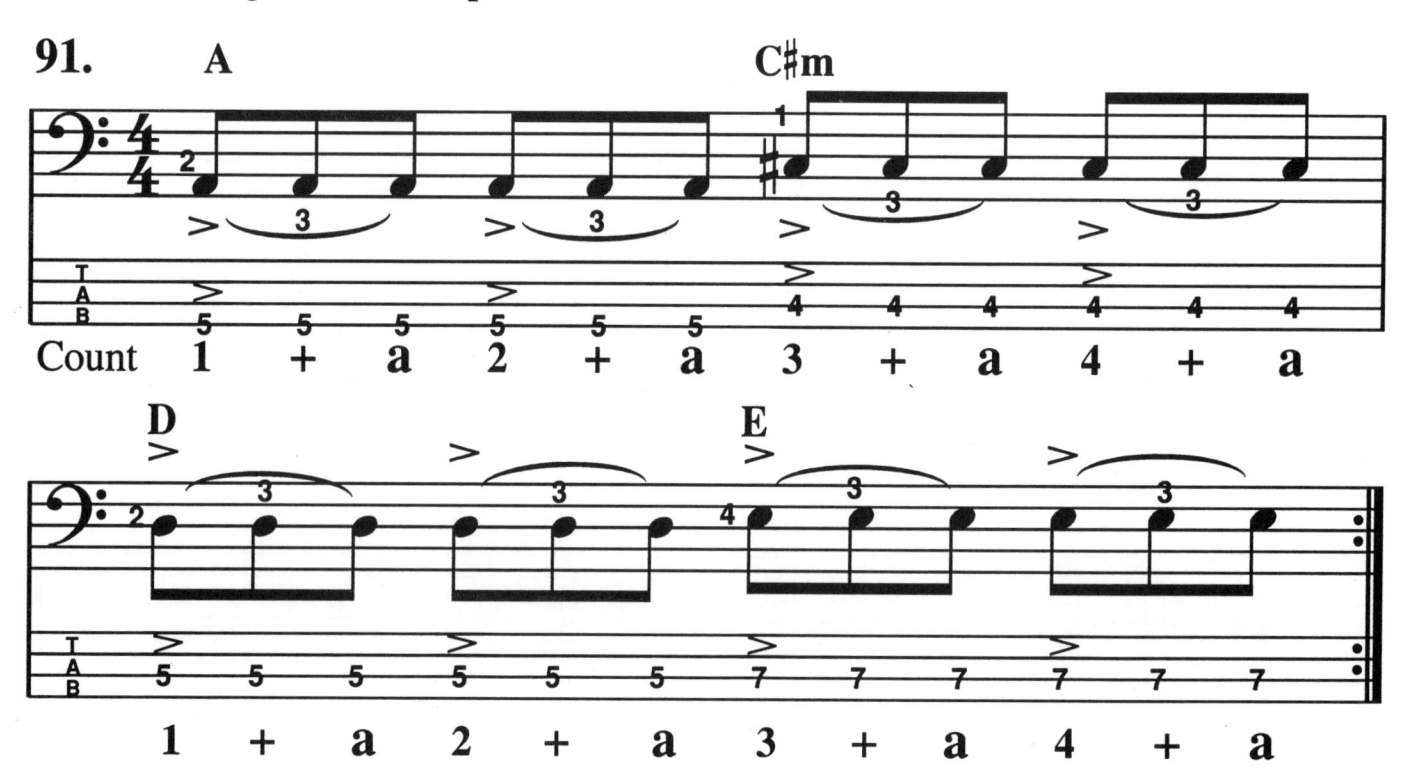

91.

Count 1 + a 2 + a 3 + a 4 + a

1 + a 2 + a 3 + a 4 + a

Shuffle Rhythm

The shuffle rhythm is a very common variation based upon the triplet. It is created by not playing the middle note of the triplet as indicated by the tie.

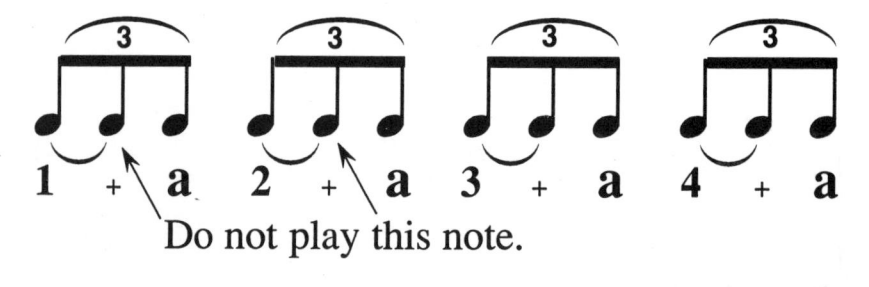

1 + a 2 + a 3 + a 4 + a
Do not play this note.

This can also be written as:

1 + a 2 + a 3 + a 4 + a

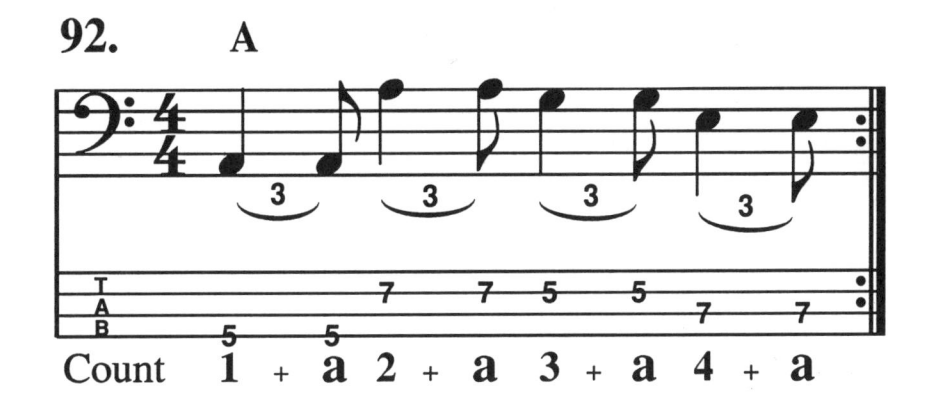

A staccato feel can be achieved by playing a rest on the middle count of the triplet, as such:

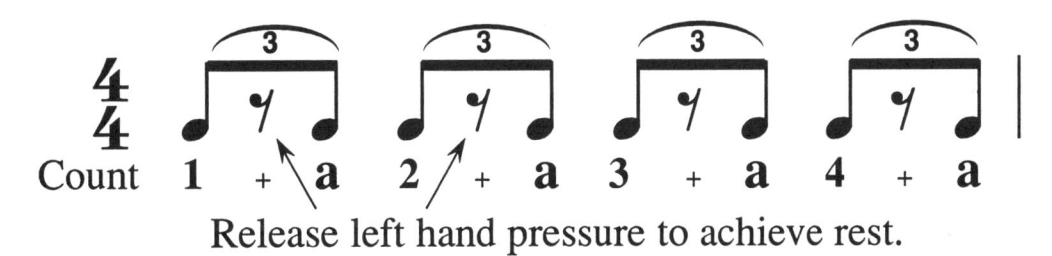

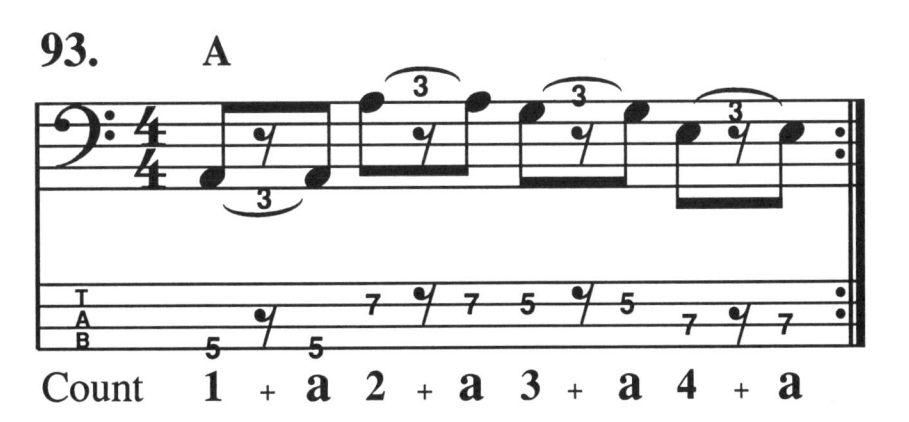

Release left hand pressure to achieve rest.

95.

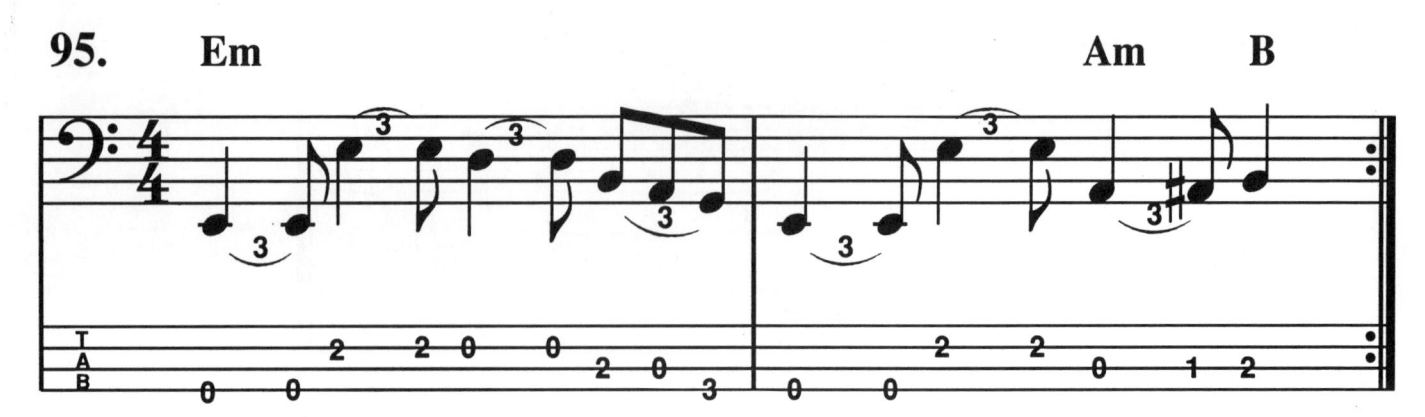

Example 96 uses a triplet feel. For the rest, mute the string with your left hand, but still maintain the triplet feel.

96.

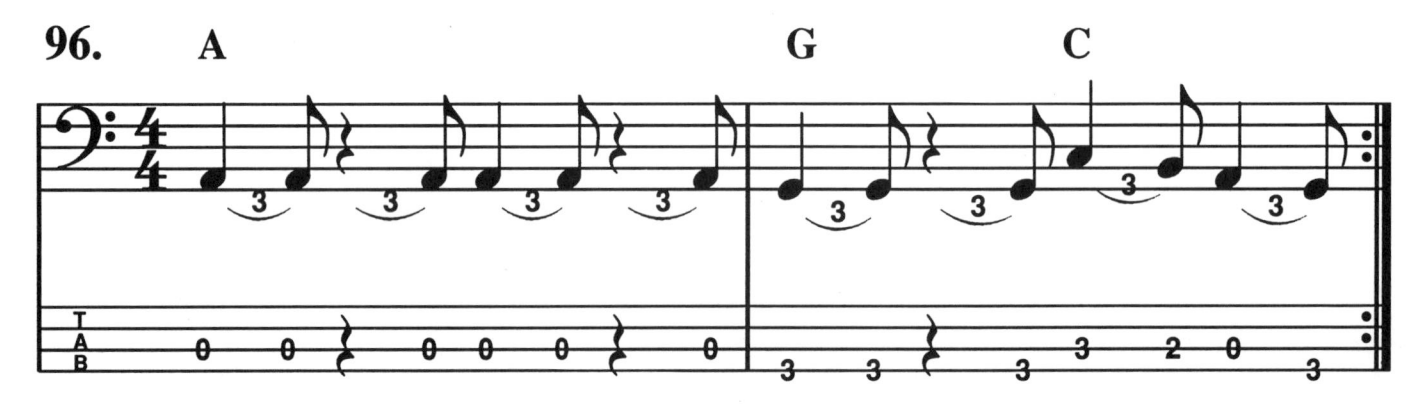

Lick 97 uses quarter notes and triplets.

97.

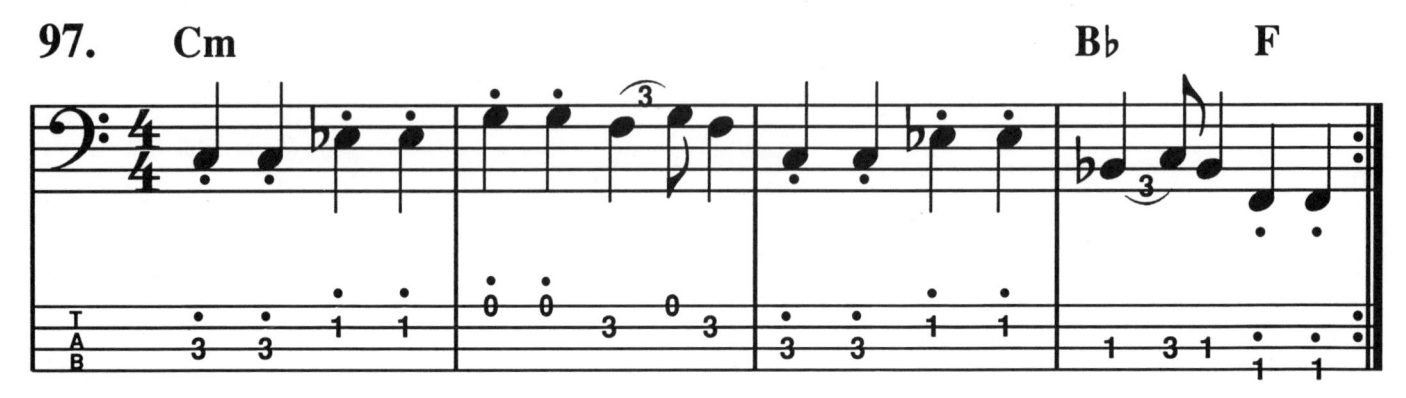

The next example uses triplets and ties.

98.

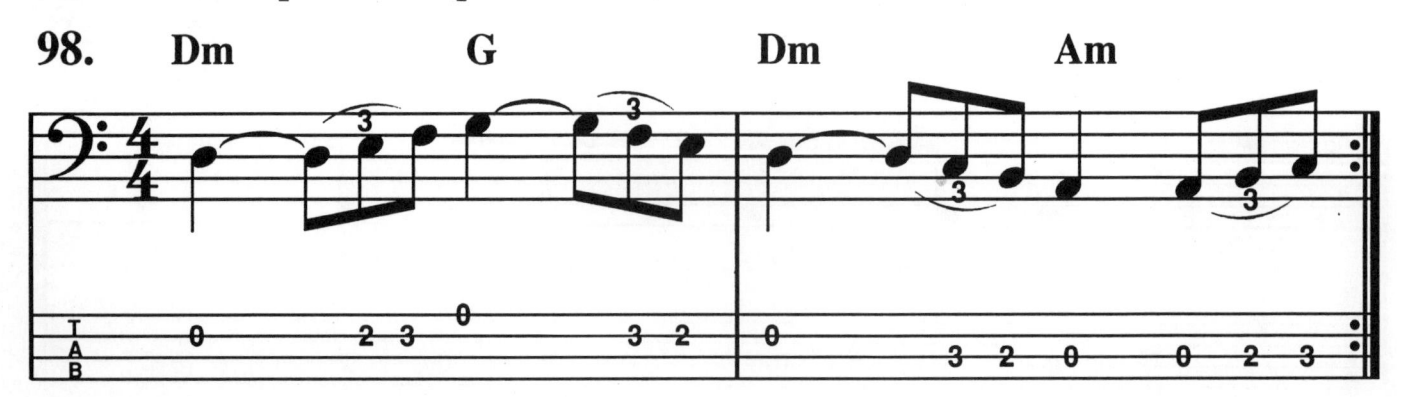

The Quarter Note Triplet

In quarter note triplet timing there are 3 quarter notes played in the space of two beats. Listen to the tape for the correct timing. The next lick uses eighth note and quarter note triplets.

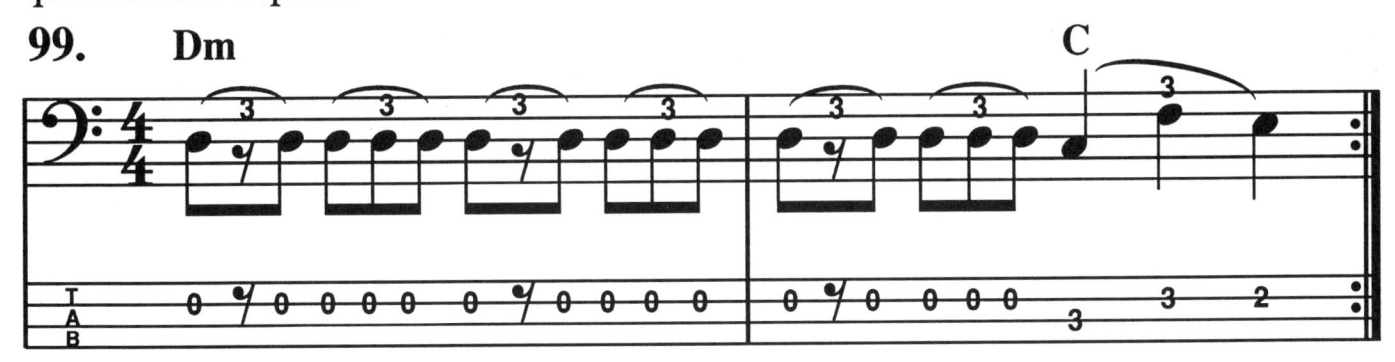

99.

In Lick 100 the first section is played three times (as indicated by *3x*) before playing the last two bars.

100.

The next example uses quarter notes, quarter note triplets and syncopation. Be careful to get your timing right.

101.

The Slide (Marked S and ⌒)

The slide is a technique which involves a finger moving along the string to its new note. The finger maintains pressure on the string, so that a continuous sound is produced until the desired note is reached. The left hand moves from one note to the next, upwards or downwards on the fretboard. If there is a curved line ⌣ underneath the note, only the first note is picked. The second one is entirely produced by the left hand finger sliding up or down the fretboard.

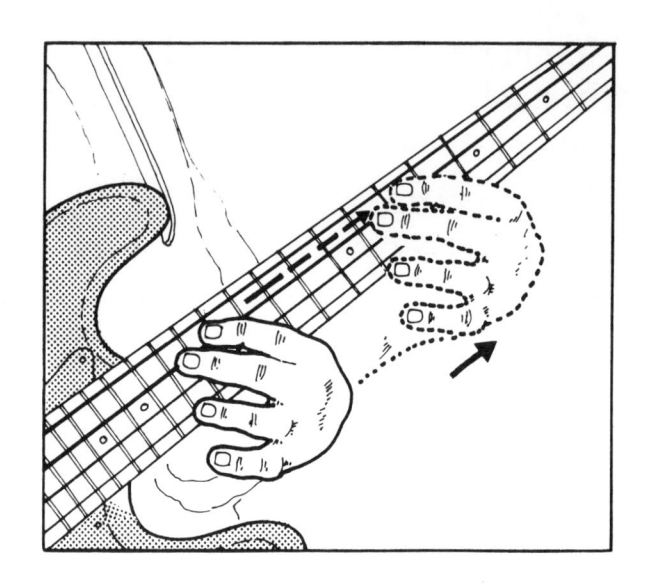

In the example below, only the first note of the slide is picked.

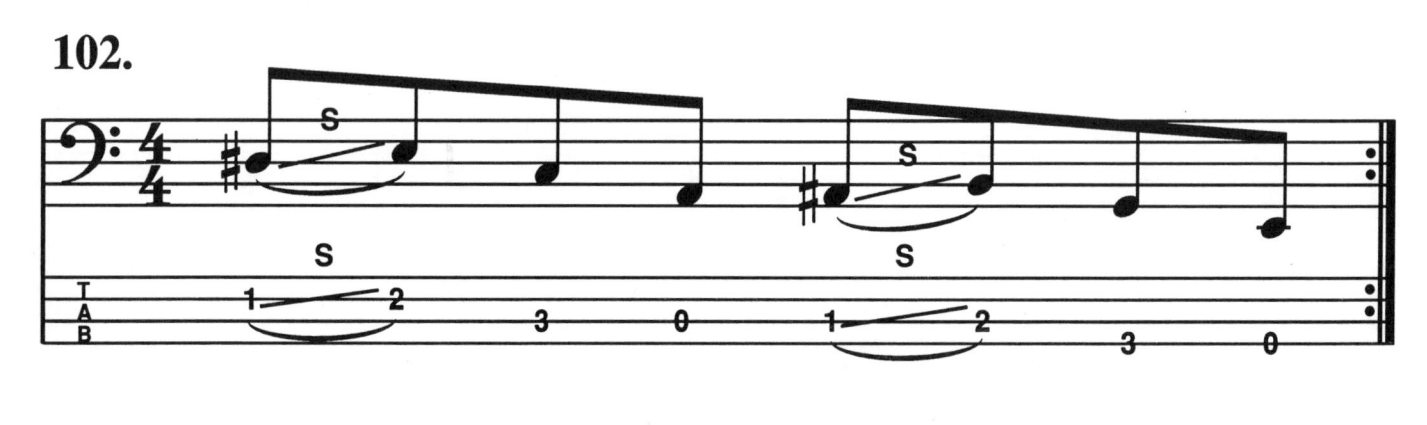

102.

103.

Pick the first E note, slide down to the low open E and pick it again.

104.

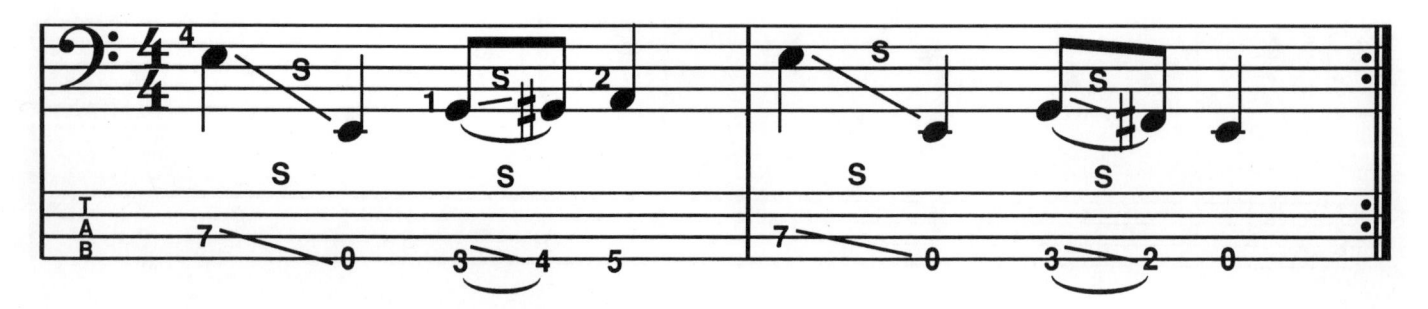

Sixteenth Notes

In music notation, a sixteenth note has the value of half an eighth note and is written as such:

Thus two sixteenth notes equal one eighth note, and four sixteenth notes equal a quarter note.

1 e + a

Say: "one e and a"

The syllables "**1e+a**" are used to represent the sixteenth note count. Here is a lick using sixteenth notes on the first three beats of the bar.

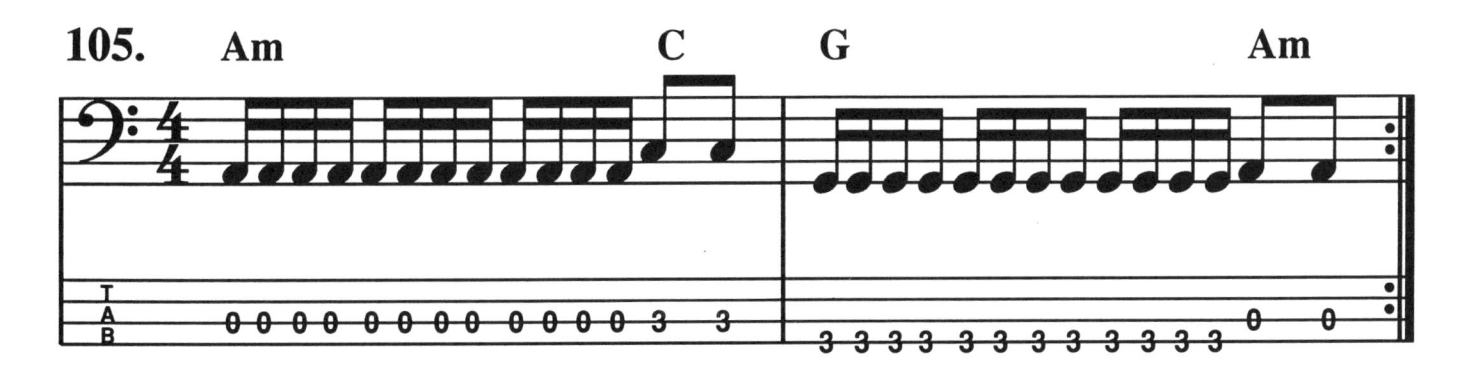

105.

106.

The Hammer-on (H)

A "hammer-on" refers to the technique of sounding a note without actually picking the string (with the pick or the right hand). The sound is produced by striking the string with one of the left hand fingers. In the exercise below, only the D note is picked, and the third finger "hammers-on" firmly to produce the sound of the E note.

107.

The hammer-on effect is indicated by the curved line, and the "H" above the note in question. Remember that the second note (E), is not picked; the sound is produced entirely by the third finger "hammering-on" to the string. You must be very careful with the timing of the hammer-on. Both the D and E notes are eighth notes and each should have an equal time value when played (regardless of the hammer-on technique).

Lick 108 is the same as Lick 106 except it is played using the "hammer-on" technique.

108.

To create a different feel with the hammer-on it can be played faster. Compare the following:

Slow Hammer-on Count 1 +

Quick Hammer-on Count 1

In Lick 109 the E note is played immediately after the D note.

109.

The quick hammer-on is applied to the first two beats which also has quarter note triplets.

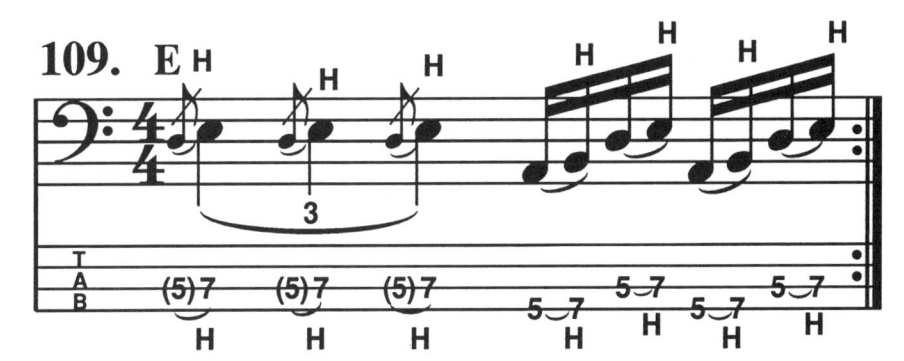

110.

Example 110 uses the quick hammer-on.

111.

Lick 111 uses hammer-on on the open D string.

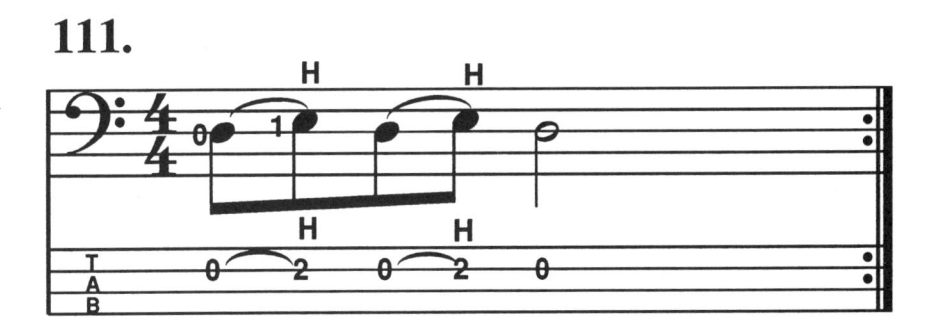

112.

Lick 112 uses an ascending hammer-on run in E minor.

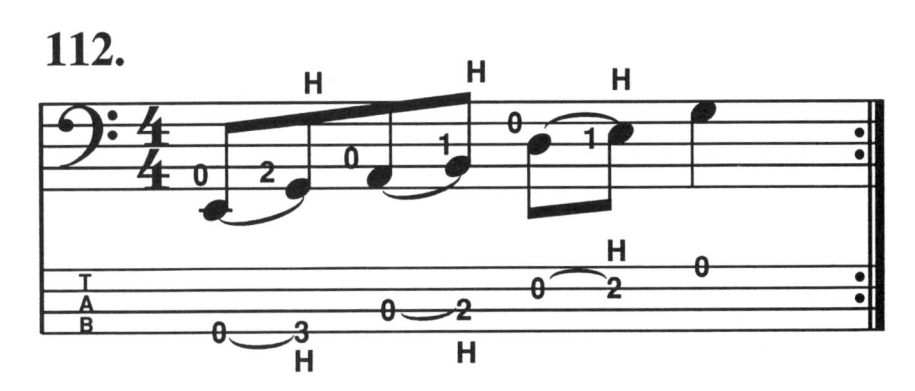

The Slap Technique

Hit the thumb against the string close to the fingerboard rapidly and firmly, twisting the wrist then releasing the thumb immediately after contact with the string. This rhythmic attack is characteristic to slap playing and is one of the selection of sounds that create the complete slap.

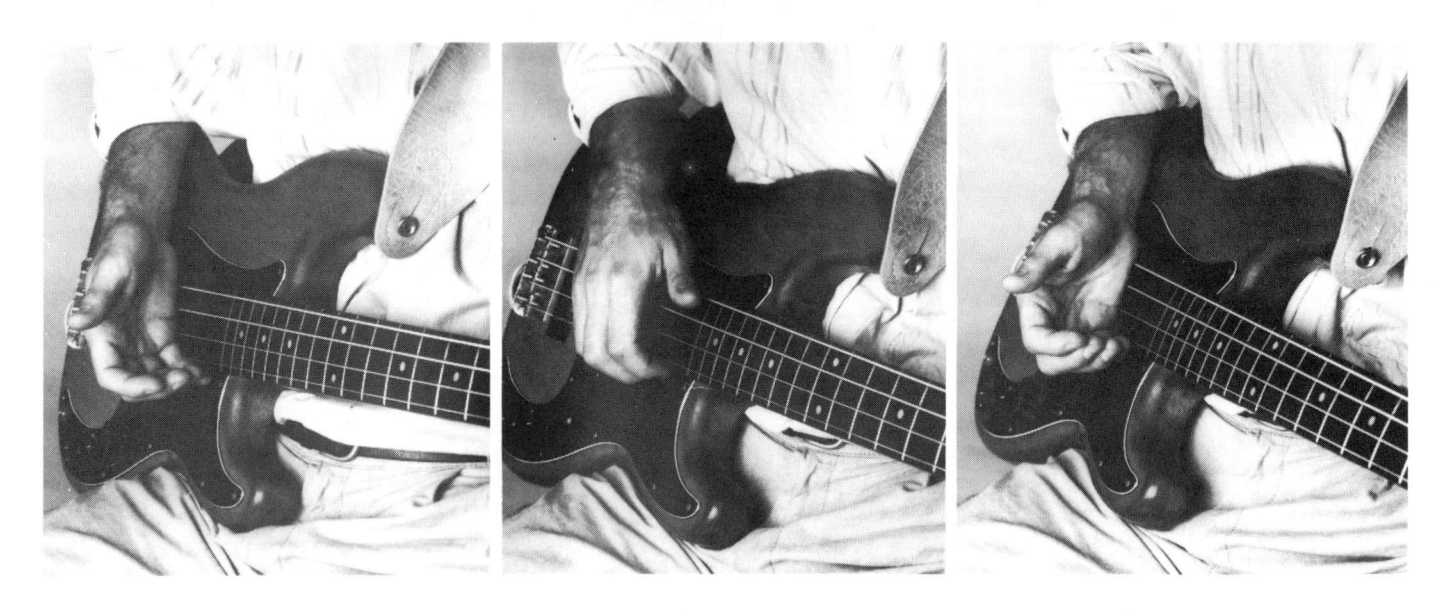

A long sustained note plays an important role in the outcome of the sound. It is achieved by the accuracy and firmness of the movement not by the force used. Smashing the string will not produce a clear sound and will in fact create unwanted background noise. For more information see *Progressive Slap Technique for Bass Guitar* by Stephan Richter.

The Tapping Technique (right hand)

Instead of picking a note, the right hand finger(s) creates the whole sound of the note(s) by hitting firmly onto the fretboard (see photo below). For more information, see *Progressive Tapping Technique for Bass*.

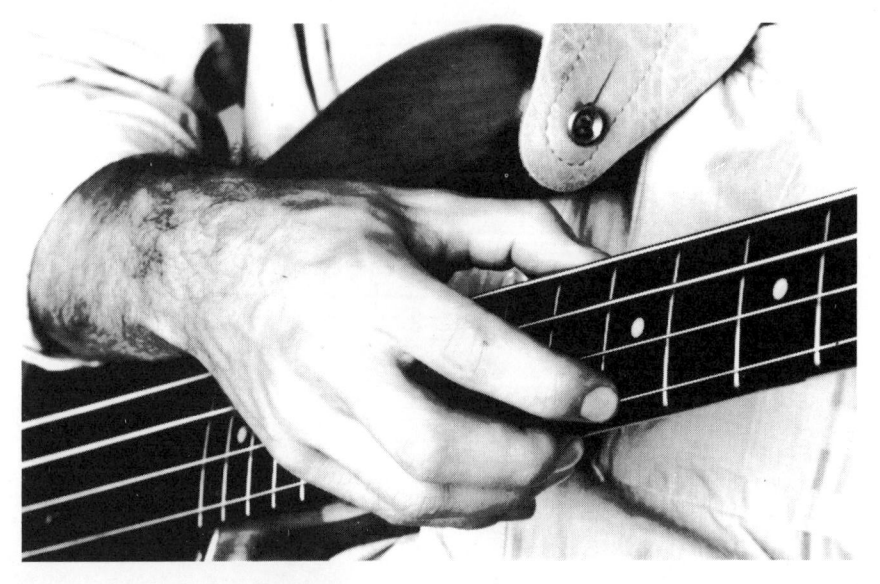

APPENDIX
Tuning

It is essential for your bass to be in tune, so that the notes you play will sound correct. The main problem with tuning for most beginning bass players is that the ear is not able to determine slight differences in pitch. For this reason you should seek the aid of a teacher or an experienced bass player.

Several methods can be used to tune the bass. These include:

1. Tuning to another musical instrument (e.g. a piano, or another guitar).
2. Tuning to a tuning fork or electronic tuner.
3. Tuning the bass to itself.

The most common and useful of these is the latter; tuning the bass to itself. This method involves finding notes of the same pitch on different strings. The diagram below outlines the notes used:

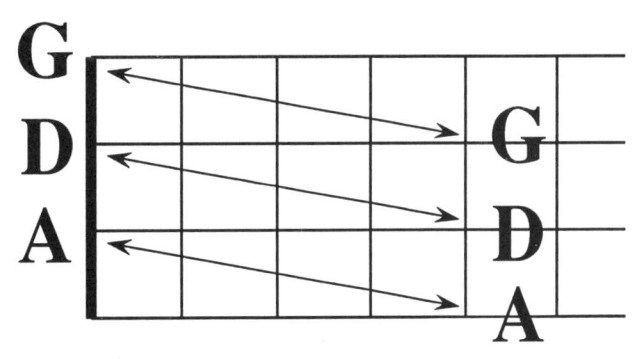

The method of tuning is as follows:

1. Tune the open 4th string to either:

    (a) The open 4th string of another bass.

    (b) A guitar.

    (c) A piano.

On the guitar, the lowest strings correspond to the 4 strings of the bass. (i.e. EADG), but are an octave higher.

On the piano, the notes equivalent to the open four strings are indicated on the diagram below.

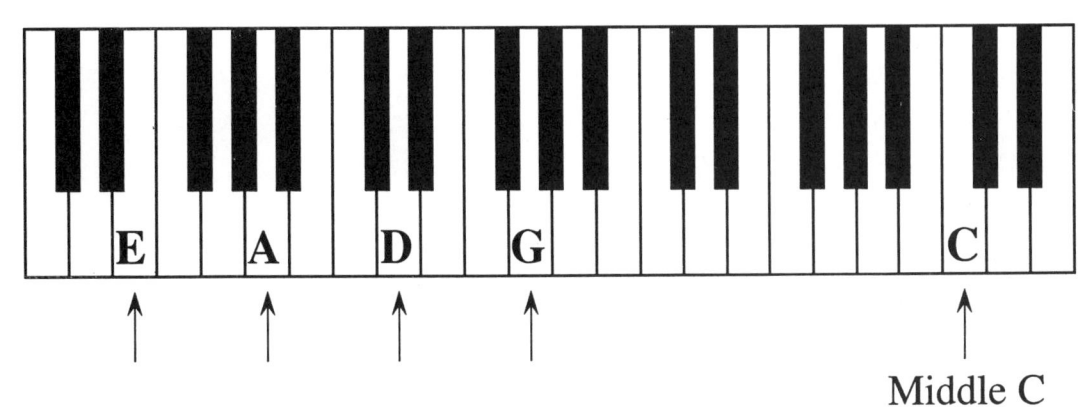

Middle C

2. Place a finger on the 4th string at the 5th fret. Now play the open A 3rd string. If the bass is to be in tune, then these two notes must have the same pitch (i.e. sound the same). If they do not sound the same, the 3rd string must be adjusted to match the note produced on the 4th string, i.e. it is tuned in relation to the 4th string.

3. Tune the open 2nd string to the note on the 5th fret of the 3rd string, using the method outlined above.

4. Tune the open 1st string to the note on the 5th fret of the second string.

Tuning Hints

One of the easiest ways to practice tuning is to actually start with the bass in tune and then de-tune one string. When you do this, always take the string down in pitch (i.e. loosen it) as it is easier to tune "up" to a given note rather than "down" to it. As an example, de-tune the 2nd string (D). If you play a riff or scale now, the bass will sound out of tune, even though only one string has been altered (so remember that if your bass is out of tune it may only be one string at fault.)

Following the correct method, you must tune the 2nd string against the D note at the 5th fret of the 3rd string. Play the note loudly, and listen carefully to the sound produced. This will help you retain the correct pitch in your mind when tuning the next string.

Now that you have listened carefully to the note that you want, the D string must be tuned to it. Pluck the D string, and turn its tuning key at the same time, and you will hear the pitch of the string change (it will become higher as the tuning key tightens the string). It is important to follow this procedure, so that you hear the sound of the string at all times, as it tightens. You should also constantly refer back to the correct sound that is required (i.e. the D note on the 5th fret of the 3rd string).

Electronic Tuners

Electronic Tuners make tuning your bass guitar very easy. They indicate the exact pitch of the string. It is still recommended however, that you practice tuning your bass guitar by the above method to help improve your musicianship.

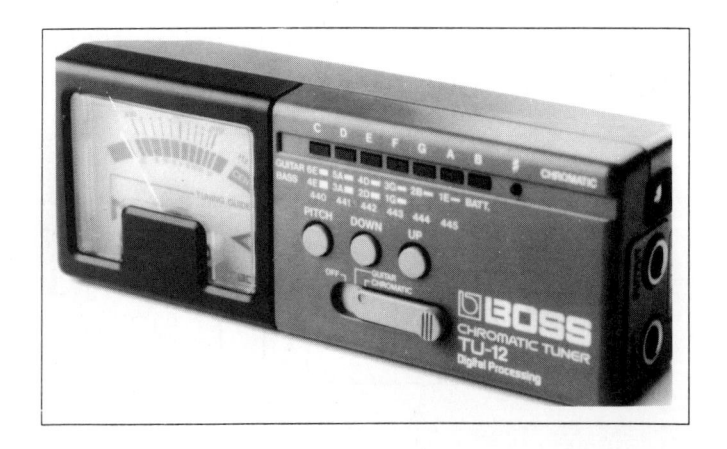

The Bass Guitar

The most important thing about a bass guitar is how it feels in your hands before you even think of plugging it into an amp.

Mechanical Check List:

- Is the weight too heavy or unbalanced? Use a strap and adjust it to the right length so that your arms and hands feel comfortable whether you stand or sit while you play.

- What is the distance (action) between the strings and the fretboard? If it is too high it is very hard to press the notes down. It can be adjusted on the bridge. If the action is too low you get a "fret buzz". Get your instrument adjusted ("set-up") by a guitar repair man.

- Does the neck sit tightly on the body? Is is straight?

– Do the tuning pegs turn easily?

Electronic Check List:

– Is the bass equipped with one or two pick ups?

– Is it active (i.e. with battery) or passive?

– Passive electronic is probably easier and more reliable than active (electronic) because of the simplicity. Active has the advantage of being more powerful and having more sound variety. Sometimes there are basses where you can switch from active to passive. Active basses use a small 9V battery which has to be put in the body normally by removing a back plate.

If the active bass has a distorted sound it could be that the signal is too high, so you have to turn your master volume back on your bass or the battery could be flat.

Strings

Different strings can be used to create different sounds and feels. Round wound strings are the most popular strings for modern bass playing.

The gauge varies between light, medium and heavy. A standard medium gauge would probably be the best to start with e.g. G = 45, D = 60, A = 80, E = 105

The heavier or thicker the gauge the "bigger" the sound will be. The lighter the strings the easier and faster you can play.

Always clean your strings with a cloth after playing as this will keep the sound brighter. To get an optimal sound, and if you can afford it, change your strings, several times a year, especially before an important session or recording.

The Bass Amp System

There are basically two different systems: 1. The Combo 2. Separate Amp and Speaker.

The Bass Combo

The Bass Combo is a very compact and convenient system. It is relatively small and easy to transport as the amp and the speaker are in one unit. You can use it for practicing at home and rehearsals and on gigs which are not too loud or big. The combo is reasonably cheap but does not have a high power output.

Separate Amp and Speaker Box(es)

There are two types of amps: the transistor and the valve amp.

The transistor amp is more neutral without distortion. The valve has a more dynamic and warmer sound and is also more expensive. The maintenance of a transistor amp is practically nothing, whereas the valve amp needs to have the valves replaced from time to time.

The power of the amp is also quite important to help get a clean strong dynamic sound. The more Watts the better because you don't need to drive your amp very hard. This gives a better sound. A 100W amp is the minimum you should use and, when on stage, 200W or more. Again the biggest problem will be the cost involved.

The Speakers

There are basically four sizes of bass speakers – 10 inch, 12 inch, 15 inch and 18 inch. Some speaker units have just one speaker. Probably the most popular all-round bass speaker is the 15 inch. It delivers the whole range of the bass sound spectrum.

However some speaker units contain several speakers and a crossover which divides the sound into lows and highs (like on a stereo system). They are bigger and heavier to transport.

Another way is to have different speaker cabinets for more versatility e.g. One 15 inch cabinet and another one with 2 or 4 10 inch speakers (for the top end sounds).

The 18 inch speaker is for super low bass sound and needs a very big cabinet. It is only suitable in conjunction with other speakers, big high power amps and for big gigs.

Sounds and Effects

There is a wide range of effects available from simple foot pedals for one particular sound up to multi-effect rack which you connect together with your amp.

What, how and when to use an effect is a matter of experience and taste, depending on the function the bass has in a particular music piece; groove or solo. Start with a neutral clean sound and experiment with that by changing the tone. E.g. boost the low end (bass boost) and the top end (treble boost) and take the mid-range back to give more sound definition.

The Equalizer

The Equalizer is a useful effect to balance your sound out, especially when you have some uneven sounding notes. You can either make them stronger by boosting a particular frequency or to reduce an overpowering sound. Some more sophisticated amps have an inbuilt E.Q.

Reverb

Reverb is a great effect to create an open space effect and works well in conjunction with most other effects. Be careful not to add too much reverb as it makes the whole sound too distant and loses definition.

Distortion

Distortion is mostly used by guitar players for lead playing. Never use it when you play a groove! Use it **very** sparingly only when there is a suitable spot for it – maybe only once in a gig.

The Volume Pedal

The volume pedal is the best effect to use if you are really interested in dynamic playing, because you can come out of nowhere up to full volume and back. It is the same idea as the volume control on your bass, but is controlled by your foot while you play.

The Compressor

The compressor evens out your dynamics. It has almost the opposite effect of a volume pedal and is very useful if you have to play very evenly and steadily especially with slapping or tapping techniques.

The Octave Divider

The octave divider adds a lower octave to the note you are playing. So when you play one note on your bass guitar, two notes sound. This effect is only useful for the higher notes on the bass guitar as the lower notes will sound too "muddy".

Chorus

The chorus pedal gives a "swirling stereo" effect on the notes you play. Best suited for solo and melody playing.

Digital Delay

The digital delay creates an echo. This echo can be adjusted to be louder or softer than the original note played. It can also be set as a short echo (a reverb effect) or a long echo which repeats the notes over and over.

There are many other effects pedals and new or modified effects appear regularly.

Playing in a Band

Probably the most important thing about playing any style or technique on the bass is to be able to fit in together with the other musicians in the band. It requires a lot of discipline when you practice alone to get your playing really "tight". Therefore practicing with a Metronome, drum machine or backing tape is essential. Without that your timing may not be strong enough and it won't hold the band together. So get together with a drummer and practice the licks and techniques with him/her until it sounds tight. Then get a guitar player who is interested in the same music and jam together with him/her. So you will then have the basic "rhythm section" which is the core of every band.

The next step is to find a singer and a lead player (keyboard, lead guitar). Get together with different people until you find the ones who fit in best with what you want to play and sound like. Listen to other players, live bands and records. The fastest way to improve your bass playing is to play with other musicians.